# THE SECULAR REASONS why America should be under God

## William J. Federer

★★ Includes Excerpts from ★★
Inaugural addresses & state constitutions

# THREE
# SECULAR
## SEASONS
### why
# America
### should be
# under
# God

# William J. Federer

★★ **Includes Excerpts from** ★★
**Inaugural addresses & state constitutions**

**Three Secular Reasons Why America Should be Under God
by William J. Federer**

To duplicate larger portions, please contact: wjfederer@aol.com, P.O. Box 4363, St. Louis, MO 63123, 314-487-4395, 314-487-4489 fax, www.amerisearch.net 1-888-USA-WORD voice/fax

HISTORY / EDUCATION    ISBN 0-9653557-9-9

Pictures Courtesy of:
Dwight Eisenhower - 1956-Wide World; Clarence Manion and Dwight Eisenhower - University of Notre Dame archives http://www. archives.nd.edu/photos/02C-032.htm; Jefferson - Rembrandt Peale 1805-New York Historical Society; Alexander Hamilton - John Trumbell, The White House Collection; JFK-Rapho-Guillumette Ted Spiegel; Truman - photograph by Fritz Henle-Photo Researchers; Coolidge - Philip de Laszlo-John Coolidge Collection; Truman - http://www.cia.gov/csi/ monograph/firstln/955pres12.gif; Daniel Webster - Richard Francis Nagle, , U.S. Senate collection, http://www.senate.gov/artandhistory/art/resources/ graphic/xlarge/32_00001.jpg; Calvin Coolidge - Blake Linton Wilfong a.k.a. The Wondersmith! http://wondersmith.com/clipart/presidents/ calvin1.gif; William Henry Harrison --daguerreotype-Metropolitan Museum of Art  Phelps-Stokes Collection; William Howard Taft - 1909 Joaquin Sorolla y Bastida-Taft Museum; James McHenry - The Constitution Society, http://www.constitution.org/img/james_mchenry.jpg; Francis Wayland - engraving by J.C. Buttre, Smithsonian Institute Archives, http:// www.sil.si.edu/Exhibitions/Smithson-to-Smithsonian/images/download/ img0045_hires.jpg; Robert Charles Winthrop - Biographical Directory of the United States Congress, http://bioguide.congress.gov/scripts/biodisplay. pl?index=W000646; Edmund Burke - http://digital.library.upenn.edu/women/ hill/burney/p182f.gif; Benjamin Franklin - Chicagp Historical Society; John Adams - Eliphalet Frazer Andrews, http://www.senate.gov/artandhistory/ art/artifact/Painting_31_00005.htm; Sir William Blackstone - http://www. ebookcdrom.com/blackstone/; Pennsylvania Supreme Court Chamber - http://www.courts.state.pa.us/Index/Supreme/photogallery6.asp; Ronald Wilson Reagan - Library of Congress; William Holmes McGuffey's Fifth Eclectic Reader.

Amerisearch, Inc., P.O. Box 20163, St. Louis, MO 63123,
1-888-USA-WORD, 314-487-4395 voice/fax
www.amerisearch.net, wjfederer@aol.com

Dedicated

to

James Mbowe Nyondo

for his tireless

effort as a

builder

of the

nation

of

Malawi

# Table
# of
# Contents

# Introduction

Do you like having rights the government cannot take away? Do you like being equal? Do you like living in a country with few laws?

If so, then you want America to be "under God" whether or not you believe in God.

In 2004, Michael Newdow filed a lawsuit in California to remove the phrase "under God" from the Pledge of Allegiance contrary to the beliefs of most Americans:

> *Gallup Poll* (2007) reported "9 in 10 Americans believe in God";
> *Harris Poll* (2003) reported 90 percent of Americans believe in God;
> *Newsweek* poll (2007) reported 91 percent of Americans believe in God; and
> *Fox News* poll (2004) reported 92 percent of Americans believe in God.
> *USA Today* (Feb. 25, 2008) reported Pew Forum's U.S. Religious Landscape Survey that only 1.6 percent of Americans are atheist.

Though much media coverage is given to the minority of atheists who want to force their views on the majority, this book examines the reasons America's founders referenced God and the implications if these references are removed.

*"The rights of man come not
from the generosity of the state,
but from the hand of God."*

**- President John F. Kennedy,
1961, Inaugural Address**

# RIGHTS

*"Nobly defend those rights which Heaven gave and no man ought to take from us."*
- Massachusetts Provincial Congress, 1774, Resolution to the inhabitants of Massachusetts Bay[1]

Do you like having rights the government cannot take away?

If you do, then those rights must come to you from a power "higher" than government.

The Declaration states "all Men are created equal, that they are endowed by their Creator with certain unalienable Rights."[2]

Dwight D. Eisenhower, in an article printed in the Episcopal Churchnews Magazine, stated:

> The founding fathers had to refer to the Creator in order to make their revolutionary experiment make sense.
>
> It was because "all men are endowed by their Creator with certain inalienable rights" that men could dare to be free.[3]

*"The founding fathers had to refer to the Creator in order to make their revolutionary experiment make sense."*

**- President Dwight Eisenhower**

# WHY GOVERNMENT EXISTS?

The Declaration states: "All Men...are endowed by their Creator with certain unalienable Rights...That to secure these Rights, Governments are instituted among Men"[4]

In other words, your rights come from God and the government exists to protect your rights.

Clarence E. Manion, Professor of Constitutional Law and dean of the Notre Dame College of Law, was quoted in Verne Paul Kaub's book, Collectivism Challenges Christianity, 1946:

> Look closely at these self-evident truths, these imperishable articles of American Faith upon which all our government is firmly based.
>
> First and foremost is the existence of God.
>
> Next comes the truth that all men are equal in the sight of God.
>
> Third is the fact of God's great gift of unalienable rights to every person on earth.
>
> Then follows the true and single purpose of all American Government, namely, to preserve and protect these God-made rights of God-made man.[5]

President Dwight Eisenhower with
Dean Clarence Manion

*"Then follows the true and
single purpose of all American
Government, namely, to preserve
and protect these God-made rights
of God-made man."*

**- Clarence E. Manion,
Professor of Constitutional
Law & Dean of the Notre Dame
College of Law**

# GIFT OF GOD

In 1781, Thomas Jefferson stated in Query XVIII of his *Notes on the State of Virginia*, portions of which are engraved on the Jefferson Memorial in Washington, D.C.:

God who gave us life gave us liberty. And can the liberties of a nation be thought secure when we have removed their only firm basis, a conviction in the minds of the people that these liberties are of the Gift of God?

That they are not to be violated but with His wrath? Indeed, I tremble for my country when I reflect that God is just; that His justice cannot sleep forever.[6]

In February of 1775, Alexander Hamilton wrote in The Farmer Refuted:

The sacred rights of mankind are not to be rummaged for among old parchments or musty records.

They are written, as with a sunbeam, in the whole volume of human nature, by the Hand of the Divinity itself, and can never be erased or obscured by mortal power.[7]

**"Can the liberties of a nation be thought secure when we have removed their only firm basis, a conviction in the minds of the people that these liberties are the Gift of God?"**

-Thomas Jefferson,
1781,
*Notes on the State of Virginia*

President Calvin Coolidge, unveiling the Equestrian Statue of Bishop Francis Asbury, Washington, D.C., October 15, 1924, stated:

Our government rests upon religion. It is from that source that we derive our reverence for truth and justice, for equality and liberty, and for the rights of mankind.

Unless the people believe in these principles they cannot believe in our government.[8]

### IF NO GOD?

If there is no God, where do rights come from? President Eisenhower addressed the American Legion's Back-to-God Program, February 20, 1955:

The Founding Fathers... recognizing God as the author of individual rights, declared that the purpose of government is to secure those rights...

In many lands the State claims to be the author of human rights...If the State gives rights, it can - and inevitably will - take away those rights.

In his Inaugural Address, 1961, President John F. Kennedy stated:

*"The sacred rights of mankind are...written...by the Hand of the Divinity itself, and can never be erased or obscured by mortal power."*

**- Alexander Hamilton, February 1775, *The Farmer Refuted***

> The rights of man come not
> from the generosity of the state, but
> from the hand of God.[9]

If there is no God, your rights cannot come from anywhere else except from the "generosity of the State." The State, then, becomes the new god. And what the State "giveth," the State can "taketh awayeth."

This was espoused by German philosopher George Wihelm Friedrich Hegel, who influenced Karl Marx and Adolf Hitler.

Hegel did not believe in the existence of God and thought the closest anyone could come to attaining "eternal life" was to create a government that would exist after their death.

Thus Communism teaches that citizens exist for Government's benefit; whereas America's founders believed that Government existed for the citizens' benefit.

Without God, government transitions from being the policeman protecting your property to the policeman owning your property.

Without God, government transitions from being your servant to your master.

President Harry S Truman addressed the Attorney General's Conference, 1950:

> The fundamental basis of this
> nation's laws was given to Moses on
> the Mount.

*"If we don't have a proper
fundamental moral background,
we will finally end up with a
totalitarian government which
does not believe in rights for
anybody except the State."*

**- President Harry S Truman,
Februray 15, 1950,
Attorney General's Conference**

The fundamental basis of our Bill of Rights comes from the teachings we get from Exodus and St. Matthew, from Isaiah and St. Paul. I don't think we emphasize that enough these days.

If we don't have a proper fundamental moral background, we will finally end up with a totalitarian government which does not believe in rights for anybody except the State.[10]

Warren Gamaliel Harding stated in Washington, DC, November 12, 1921:

Inherent rights are of God, and the tragedies of the world originate in their attempted denial.[11]

Ronald Reagan, April 27, 1984, commented to the Chinese community in Beijing:

I have seen the rise of fascism and communism. Both philosophies glorify the arbitrary power of the state...But both theories fail. Both deny those God-given liberties that are the inalienable right of each person on this planet, indeed, they deny the existence of God.[12]

*"We believe that all men are created equal, because they are created in the image of God."*

- **President Harry S Truman, 1949, Inaugural Address**

# EQUALITY

*"We believe that all men are created equal, because they are created in the image of God."*
- Harry S Truman, 1949, Inaugural Address[13]

Where does the idea of equality come from? President Calvin Coolidge stated on September 21, 1924, in an address to the Holy Name Society in Washington, D.C.:

The principle of equality is recognized. It follows inevitably from belief in the brotherhood of man through the fatherhood of God...

It seems perfectly plain that the right to equality has for its foundation reverence for God.

If we could imagine that swept away our American government could not long survive.[14]

Individuals being equal before the law is based on equality before a Supreme Being, as

*"The principle of equality...*
*follows inevitably from belief in*
*the brotherhood of man through*
*the fatherhood of God."*

**- President Calvin Coolidge,**
**September 24, 1924,**
**Address to the Holy Name Society**

Franklin Roosevelt said March 16, 1940:

> The active search for peace...
> meant...overcoming those forces...
> which denied the equality of souls
> before the throne of God.[15]

President William Howard Taft stated at a missionary conference, 1908:

> The spirit of Christianity is
> pure democracy. It is equality of
> man before God - the equality of
> man before the law, which is, as I
> understand it, the most God-like
> manifestation that man has been able
> to make.[16]

Daniel Webster stated at the Bunker Hill Monument, Massachusetts, June 17, 1843:

> The Bible is a book of faith,
> and a book of doctrine, and a book
> of morals, and a book of religion,
> of special revelation from God; but
> it is also a book which teaches man
> his own individual responsibility, his
> own dignity, and his equality with
> his fellow-man.[17]

President William Henry Harrison, in his

*"The spirit of Christianity...is equality of man before God - the equality of man before the law, which is, as I understand it, the most God-like manifestation that man has been able to make."*

**- President William Howard Taft, 1908, at a missionary conference**

Inaugural Address, March 4, 1841, stated:

> Believing that so far as power is concerned the Beneficent Creator has made no distinction amongst men; that all are upon an equality.[18]

Herbert Hoover, in San Diego, California, September 17, 1935, stated:

> The American system of liberty...is based upon certain inalienable freedoms and protections which in no event the government may infringe...
> It does not require a lawyer to interpret those provisions. They are as clear as the Ten Commandments.
> Among others the freedom of worship, freedom of speech and of the press, the right of peaceable assembly, equality before the law...
> In them lies a spiritual right of men. Behind them is the conception which is the highest development of the Christian faith - the conception of individual freedom with brotherhood.[19]

President Ronald Reagan wrote in the article "Abortion and the Conscience of the

*"The Bible is a book...which teaches man...his equality with his fellow-man."*

**- Daniel Webster, June 17, 1843, Address celebrating the completion of the Bunker Hill Monument, Charleston, Massachusetts**

Nation," (*The Human Life Review*, 1983):

> When Congressman John A. Bingham of Ohio drafted the Fourteenth Amendment to guarantee the rights of life, liberty, and property to all human beings, he explained that all are "entitled to the protection of American laws, because its divine spirit of equality declares that all men are created equal."[20]

## IF NO GOD?

But if there is no God - then men are not only not "created," they are not "equal," as Charles Darwin espoused, some are "more evolved" than others. Darwin wrote in his *Descent of Man*, 1871:

> With savages, the weak in body or mind are soon eliminated...
> We civilised men, on the other hand...build asylums for the imbecile, the maimed and the sick...
> Thus the weak members propagate their kind. No one who had attended to the breeding of domestic animals will doubt that this must be highly injurious to the race of man...
> Hardly anyone is so ignorant

*"Believing that so far as power is concerned the Beneficent Creator has made no distinction amongst men; that all are upon an equality."*

**- President William Henry Harrison, March 4, 1841, Inaugural Address**

as to allow his worst animals to breed... Civilized races of man will almost certainly exterminate and replace the savage races throughout the world...

The break between man and his nearest allies will then be wider, for it will intervene between man in a more civilised state, as we may hope, even than the Caucasian, and some ape as low as a baboon, instead of as now between the negro or Australian and the gorilla.[21]

Darwin's concept provided justification for Democrat-appointed Chief Justice Roger Taney's *Dred Scott Decision*, 1856:

Slaves had for more than a century before been regarded as beings of an inferior order...so far inferior, that they had no rights which the white man was bound to respect; and that the Negro might justly and lawfully be reduced to slavery for his benefit.[22]

Darwin's concept influenced Margaret Sanger, who, prior to World War II, promoted "eugenics" and "forced sterilization" to eliminate inferior races.

*"Equality, liberty, popular sovereignty, the rights of man - these...have their source and their roots in the religious convictions....We can not continue to enjoy the result if we neglect and abandon the cause."*

**- President Calvin Coolidge, July 5, 1926, on the 150th Anniversary Celebration of the Declaration of Independence, Philadelphia**

Sanger founded Planned Parenthood which published the writing Ernst Rudin, the head of "racial hygene" for the National Socialist Workers Party (Nazi). Ernst Rudin stated:

> The significance of Rassenhygiene (racial hygiene) did not become evident to all aware Germans until the political activity of Adolf Hitler and only through his work has our 30-year long dream of translating Rassenhygiene into action finally become a reality...
>
> Whoever is not physically or mentally fit must not pass on his defects to his children. The state must take care that only the fit produce children.

In her book *Pivot of Civilization*, 1922, Margaret Sanger called for the:

> Elimination of "human weeds" ...overrunning the human garden; for the cessation of "charity" because it prolonged the lives of the unfit; for the segregation of "morons, misfits, and the maladjusted"; and for the sterilization of genetically inferior races.[23]

Sanger's "eugenics" influenced Hitler to consider the German, or "Aryan," race as "ubermensch," supermen, being more advanced in the supposed progress of human evolution.[24]

This resulted in the perverted effort to rid the "human gene pool" of Jews, considered "untermensch"- under mankind, a less evolved inferior race - through the use of gas chambers and ovens.

Joseph Stalin followed this example in the Soviet Union, exterminating by forced famines, forced labor and executions 27 million "inferior" Ukrainians.[25] Mao Zedong's atheistic Chinese Communist Party policies caused an estimated 80 million deaths.[26]

Teaching that Jews are from apes, Christians are from swine, and Kafir infidels are inferior "dhimmi" - not equal to believing Muslims - has contributed to an estimated 270 million jihad deaths in the last 1,400 years.[27]

The potential consequences are frightful if a country departs from President Truman's Judeo-Christian belief, "that all men are created equal because they are created in the image of God."[28]

## WE CANNOT ENJOY THE RESULT
## IF WE NEGLECT THE CAUSE

President Calvin Coolidge, at the 150th Anniversary of the Declaration of Independence, Philadelphia, July 5, 1926, explained how equality was not permitted in the monarchies of Europe, but developed from teachings in colonial America:

> The principles of human relationship which went into the Declaration of Independence...are found in the texts, the sermons, and the writings of the early colonial clergy who were earnestly undertaking to instruct their congregations in the great mystery of how to live.
>
> They preached equality because they believed in the fatherhood of God and the brotherhood of man.
>
> They justified freedom by the text that we are all created in the divine image, all partakers of the divine spirit....
>
> Placing every man on a plane where he acknowledged no superiors, where no one possessed any right to rule over him, he must inevitably choose his own rulers through a system of self-government...
>
> In those days such doctrines would scarcely have been permitted to flourish and spread in any other country....
>
> In order that they might have

freedom to express these thoughts and opportunity to put them into action, whole congregations with their pastors had migrated to the colonies....

In its main feature the Declaration of Independence is a great spiritual document. It is a declaration not of material but of spiritual conceptions.

Equality, liberty, popular sovereignty, the rights of man - these are...ideals. They have their source and their roots in the religious convictions. They belong to the unseen world.

Unless the faith of the American in these religious convictions is to endure, the principles of our Declaration will perish.

We can not continue to enjoy the result if we neglect and abandon the cause.[29]

# FEW LAWS

*"Our Constitution was made only for a moral and religious people. It is wholly inadequate to the government of any other."*
- John Adams, October 11, 1798, letter to the Third Division of the Militia of Massachusetts.[30]

Where does the idea of a having few laws come from?

By reviewing writings of the founders, it appears that American government was designed to govern people who could govern themselves.

John Quincy Adams, September 1811, while serving for a second time as U.S. Ministry in St. Petersburg, Russia, wrote to his son:

> So great is my veneration for the Bible...that the earlier my children begin to read it...the more lively and confident will be my hopes that they will prove useful citizens of their country...
>
> It is essential, my son, in order that you may go through life with

*"Our Constitution was made only for a moral and religious people. It is wholly inadequate to the government of any other."*

**- President John Adams, October 11, 1798, Letter to the Third Division of the Militia of Massachusetts.**

comfort to yourself, and usefulness to your fellow-creatures, that you should form and adopt certain rules or principles, for the government of your own conduct and temper....

It is in the Bible, you must learn them, and from the Bible how to practice them.

Those duties are to God, to your fellow-creatures, and to yourself.

"Thou shalt love the Lord thy God, with all thy heart, and with all thy soul, and with all thy mind, and with all thy strength, and thy neighbor as thy self."[31]

William Holmes McGuffey, president of Ohio University and professor at the University of Virginia, was the Department Chairman at Miami University of Ohio and formed the first teachers' association in that part of the nation.

His *McGuffey's Readers* were a mainstay in public education, selling over 125 million copies as of 1963. In *McGuffey's Fifth Eclectic Reader* (1879), lesson XCIII, is an essay by William Ellery Channing entitled: "Religion - The Only Basis of Society":

Religion is a social concern; for it operates powerfully, contributing

*"In order that you may go
through life with usefulness
to your fellow-creatures... you
should adopt certain rules for the
government of your own
conduct... It is in the Bible
you must learn them."*

**- John Quincy Adams,
September 1811,
U.S. Minister to Russia, Letter to his son**

in various ways to its stability and prosperity.

Religion is not merely a private affair; the community is deeply interested in its diffusion; for it is the best support of the virtues and principles, on which the social order rests.

Pure and undefiled religion is, to do good; and it follows, very plainly, that if God be the Author and Friend of Society, then, the recognition of him must enforce all social duty, and enlightened piety must give its whole strength to public order.[32]

James McHenry, signer of the U.S. Constitution and U.S. Secretary of War who supervised the establishment of West Point Military Academy, stated to the Baltimore, Maryland, Bible Society, 1813:

Public utility pleads most forcibly for the general distribution of the Holy Scriptures.

The doctrine they preach, the obligations they impose, the punishment they threaten, the rewards they promise...can alone secure to society, order and peace,

**"Without the Bible, we increase penal laws."**

**- James McHenry, Signer of the U.S. Constitution, 1813, to the Baltimore, Maryland, Bible Society**

and to our courts of justice and constitutions of government...

Without the Bible, we increase penal laws.[33]

Francis Wayland, a Harvard graduate and president of Brown University, 1827-55, was the first president of the American Institute of Instruction, 1830. He stated:

That the truths of the Bible have the power of awakening an intense moral feeling in every human being;

that they make bad men good, and send a pulse of healthful feeling through all the domestic, civil, and social relations;

that they teach men to love right, and hate wrong, and seek each other's welfare as children of a common parent;

that they control the baleful passions of the heart, and thus make men proficient in self government; and finally

that they teach man to aspire after conformity to a Being of infinite holiness, and fill him with hopes more purifying, exalted, and suited to his nature than any other

*"The truths of the Bible have the power of awakening an intense moral feeling in every human be-ing...they teach men to...seek each other's welfare as children of a common parent."*

**- Francis Wayland, president of Brown University, 1827-55, and president of the American Institute of Instruction, 1830**

book the world has ever known -

These are facts as incontrovertible as the laws of philosophy, or the demonstrations of mathematics.[34]

## INTERNAL OR EXTERNAL LAWS?

A country can get by with few external laws if the people have an internal law. This is the principle of "self-government."

Robert Winthrop, U.S. Speaker of the House in 1849, stated:

All societies of men must be governed in some way or other. The less they have of stringent State Government, the more they must have of individual self-government.

The less they rely on public law or physical force, the more they must rely on private moral restraint.

Men, in a word, must necessarily be controlled either by a power within them, or a power without them; either by the word of God, or by the strong arm of man; either by the Bible or by the bayonet.[35]

British Statesman Edmund Burke wrote to a Member of the National Assembly, 1791:

*"Men, in a word, must necessarily
be controlled either by a power
within them, or a power without
them; either by the word of God,
or by the strong
arm of man."*

**- Robert Charles Winthrop, U.S.
Speaker of the House, 1849**

What is liberty without virtue?
It is the greatest of all possible evils...
it is madness without restraint.

Men are qualified for civil liberty in exact proportion to their disposition to put moral chains upon their own appetites...

Society cannot exist, unless a controlling power upon will and appetite be placed somewhere; and the less of it there is within, the more there must be without.

It is ordained in the eternal constitution of things that men of intemperate minds cannot be free. Their passions forge their fetters (shackles).[36]

Massachusetts Governor Samuel Adams wrote to James Warren, February 12, 1779:

A general dissolution of the principles and manners will more surely overthrow the liberties of America than the whole force of the common enemy.

While the people are virtuous they cannot be subdued; but once they lose their virtue, they will be ready to surrender their liberties to the first external or internal invader.

If we would enjoy this gift of

*"Men are qualified for civil liberty in exact proportion to their disposition to put moral chains upon their own appetites...and he less of it there is within, the more there must be without."*

**- British Statesman Edmund Burke, 1791, "A Letter to a Member of the National Assembly"**

Heaven, let us become a virtuous people."[37]

William Howard Taft speaking at a missionary conference, 1908, stated:

> No man can study the movement of modern civilization from an impartial standpoint, and not realize that Christianity and the spread of Christianity are the basis of hope of modern civilization in the growth of popular self government.[38]

## FUTURE ACCOUNTABILITY

To be a country with "few laws," citizens must have an internal law for there to be order, but an internal law is powerless without a consequence, such as being held accountable to a Supreme Being in some future state.

Secretary of State Daniel Webster was asked what the greatest thought was that ever passed through his mind. He replied:

> "My accountability to God."[39]

Benjamin Franklin wrote to Yale President Ezra Stiles, March 9, 1790:

> The soul of Man is immortal,

*"The soul of Man is immortal,
and will be treated with Justice
in another Life respecting its
conduct in this."*

**- Benjamin Franklin, March 9, 1790,
writing to Yale President Ezra Stiles**

and will be treated with justice in another life respecting its conduct in this.[40]

Benjamin Franklin believed:

That there is one God, Father of the Universe...
That He loves such of His creatures as love and do good to others: and will reward them either in this world or hereafter,
That men's minds do not die with their bodies, but are made more happy or miserable after this life according to their actions.[41]

John Adams wrote to Judge F.A. Van der Kemp, January 13, 1815:

My religion is founded on the love of God and my neighbor; in the hope of pardon for my offenses; upon contrition...in the duty of doing no wrong, but all the good I can, to the creation, of which I am but an infinitesimal part.
I believe, too, in a future state of rewards and punishments.[42]

John Adams wrote to Judge F.A. Van de Kemp, December 27, 1816:

*"I believe, too, in a future state of rewards and punishments."*

**- President John Adams,
January 13, 1815,
to Judge F.A. Van der Kemp**

Let it once be revealed or demonstrated that there is no future state, and my advice to every man, woman, and child, would be, as our existence would be in our own power, to take opium.

For, I am certain there is nothing in this world worth living for but hope, and every hope will fail us, if the last hope, that of a future state, is extinguished.[43]

John Adams wrote in a Proclamation of Humiliation, Fasting, and Prayer, March 6, 1799:

No truth is more clearly taught in the Volume of Inspiration...than... acknowledgment of...a Supreme Being and of the accountableness of men to Him as the searcher of hearts and righteous distributor of rewards and punishments are conducive equally to the happiness and rectitude of individuals and to the well-being of communities.[44]

On November 25, 1862, Abraham Lincoln told Rev. Byron Sunderland of the First Presbyterian Church, Washington, DC:

I believe in the supremacy of the human conscience, and that men

*"The belief of a future state of rewards and punishments...[is] the grand foundations of all judicial oaths, which call God to witness."*

- Sir William Blackstone, 1765-1770, Commentaries on the Laws of England

are responsible beings, that God has a right to hold them, and will hold them, to a strict account for the deeds done in the body.

But, sirs, I do not mean to give you a lecture upon the doctrines of the Christian religion. These are simply with me the convictions and realities of great and vital truths.[45]

## STATE OATHS

Having few laws because citizens strive to keep an internal law, aware they will be accountable in a "future state," is seen in State Constitutions and Court Decisions.

The Constitution of Pennsylvania, 1776, Chapter 2, Section 10, stated:

Each member, before he takes his seat, shall make and subscribe the following declaration, viz:

"I do believe in one God, the Creator and Governour of the Universe, the Rewarder of the good and Punisher of the wicked, and I do acknowledge the Scriptures of the Old and New Testament to be given by Divine Inspiration."[46]

The Constitution of South Carolina, 1778, Article XII, stated:

*"Laws cannot be administered in any civilized government unless the people are taught to revere the sanctity of an oath, and look to a future state of rewards and punishments for the deeds of this life."*

**Pennsylvania Supreme Court, 1817, *Commonwealth v. Wolf*, 3 Serg. & R. 48, 50**

Every...person, who acknowledges the being of a God, and believes in the future state of rewards and punishments...[is eligible to vote].[47]

The Constitution of South Carolina, 1790, Article XXXVIII, stated:

That all persons and religious societies, who acknowledge that there is one God, and a future state of rewards and punishments, and that God is publicly to be worshipped, shall be freely tolerated.[48]

The Constitution of Mississippi, 1817, stated:

No person who denies the being of God or a future state of rewards and punishments shall hold any office in the civil department of the State.[49]

Pennsylvania's Supreme Court stated in *Commonwealth v. Wolf* (3 Serg. & R. 48, 50, 1817:

Laws cannot be administered in any civilized government unless the people are taught to revere the sanctity of an oath, and look to a future state of rewards and punishments for the deeds of this life.[50]

The Constitution of Maryland, 1851, required:

A declaration of belief in the Christian religion; and if the party shall profess to be a Jew the declaration shall be of his belief in a future state of rewards and punishments.[51]

The Constitution of Maryland, 1864, required office holders to make:

A declaration of belief in the Christian religion, or of the existence of God, and in a future state of rewards and punishments.[52]

The Constitution of Tennessee, 1870, Article IX, Section 2, stated:

No person who denies the being of God, or a future state of rewards and punishments, shall hold any office in the civil department of this State.[53]

The idea of an oath was to call a higher

power to hold you accountable to perform what you said you would.

This accountability is expressed in all three branches of government: The President's oath of office ends with "So Help Me God"; Congressmen and Senators' oath of office ends with "So Help Me God," and Federal Judges' oath of office ends with "So Help Me God."

The traditional courtroom oath for witnesses ended "to tell the truth, the whole truth and nothing but the truth, So Help Me God." The military's oath of enlistment and oath for commissioned officers ends with "So Help Me God."

Sir William Blackstone, one of the most quoted authors by America's founders, wrote in *Commentaries on the Laws of England*, 1765-1770:

> The belief of a future state of rewards and punishments, the entertaining just ideas of the main attributes of the Supreme Being, and a firm persuasion that He superintends and will finally compensate every action in human life (all which are revealed in the doctrines of our Savior, Christ),
>
> these are the grand foundations of all judicial oaths, which call God to witness the truth of those facts which perhaps may be only known to Him and the party attesting.[54]

*"Without God democracy will
not and cannot long endure....
If we ever forget that we are One
Nation Under God, then we will
be a Nation gone under."*

**- President Ronald Reagan,
August 23, 1984, Ecumenical
prayer breakfast,
Reunion Arena, Dallas**

It was known that witnesses or politicians would have opportunities to twist the truth and do dirty, backroom deals for their own benefit and never get caught.

But it was reasoned that if a witness or politician believed God existed and was looking over their shoulder, they would hesitate when presented with the temptation. They would have a conscience.

They would think twice before giving in, considering "even if I get away with this unscrupulous action in this life, I will still be accountable to God in the next."

But if that person did not believe in God and in a future state of rewards and punishments, when presented with the same temptation to do wrong and not get caught, they would give in.

In fact, if there is no God and this life is all there is, they would be a fool not to.

## CONSCIENCE

President Reagan referred to this while speaking on the Equal Access Bill in Dallas, Texas, August 23, 1984:

> Without God there is no virtue because there is no prompting of the conscience.[55]

William Linn was unanimously elected the first Chaplain of the U.S. House, May 1, 1789, He stated:

> Let my neighbor once persuade himself that there is no God, and he will soon pick my pocket, and break not only my leg but my neck.
>
> If there be no God, there is no law, no future account; government then is the ordinance of man only, and we cannot be subject for conscience sake.[56]

Linn's observation was demonstrated when, after 80 years of atheism, the countries of the former Soviet Union were given liberty, and the result was that organized crime and the black market took significant control.

From Bill Clinton to Enron Corporation, one sees where the absence of an internal law will take a country - crimes are only wrong if one gets caught.

Unfortunately, the less internal moral code a nation has results in the government having to pass more external legal codes to keep order - and each new law takes away another little piece of individual freedom.

*McGuffey's Fifth Eclectic Reader* (Cincinnati & NY: Van Antwerp, Bragg & Co., 1879), included lesson XCIII, "Religion The Only Basis of Society" by William Ellery Channing:

How powerless conscience would become without the belief of a God...Erase all thought and fear of God from a community, and selfishness and sensuality would absorb the whole man.

Appetite, knowing no restraint, and suffering, having no solace or hope, would trample in scorn on the restraints of human laws.

Virtue, duty, principle, would be mocked and spurned as unmeaning sounds.

A sordid self-interest would supplant every feeling; and man would become, in fact, what the theory in atheism declares him to be, - a companion for brutes.[57]

Patrick Henry noted:

It is when a people forget God that tyrants forge their chains...A corrupted public conscience is incompatible with freedom.[58]

John Adams wrote to Jefferson, April 19, 1817:

Without religion, this world would be something not fit to be mentioned in polite company....

The most abandoned scoundrel that ever existed, never yet wholly extinguished his Conscience and while Conscience remains, there is some religion.[59]

General Omar Bradley stated in his address on Armistice Day, November 11, 1948:

We have grasped the mystery of the atom and rejected the Sermon on the Mount....
The world has achieved brilliance without conscience. Ours is a world of nuclear giants and ethical infants.[60]

U.S. Supreme Court Justice James Wilson, who was appointed by George Washington, wrote:

The eminent distinction between right and wrong...[is revealed] by our conscience, by our reason, and by the Holy Scriptures.[61]

In 1745, copying the *110 Rules of Civility,* George Washington wrote:

Labor to keep alive in your breast that little spark of Celestial fire called Conscience.[62]

# WHOSE BELIEF SYSTEM?

The ACLU, Americans United for the Separation of Church and State, Free Thinkers, and like groups, want "under God" out of the Pledge,[63] Ten Commandments removed from public,[64] school prayer prohibited,[65] soldiers to stop saying "God Bless you" at military funerals,[66] and librarians fired for wearing cross necklaces.[67]

At the same time, the vast majority of cases taken by the ACLU defend a right to abortion,[68] to publish pornography,[69] to practice polygamy,[70] and to protect the free speech of groups like the North American Man-Boy Love Association.[71]

It is clear these groups have an agenda. They say they simply want the government neutral with regards to "religion," and their argument sounds reasonable...until one looks up the definition of the word "religion."

*Random House Unabridged Dictionary of the English Language* defines "religion" as: "a set of beliefs."[72] *Webster's New World Dictionary* defines "religion" as: "a system of belief."[73]

The word "belief" is defined as opinions, convictions - thoughts upon which one bases their actions.[74]

Thus, it follows, that as long as a person is doing "actions," they have thoughts preceding those actions - and that collection of thoughts is that person's "system of belief" or "religion."

As long as the government is doing "actions," the government has thoughts preceding those actions - and that collection of thoughts is the government's "system of belief" or "religion."

So there can never really be a separation of "religion" and government - as long as the government is doing "actions" there are thoughts, convictions and beliefs underlying those actions.

The ACLU is not being "religion" neutral, but rather it is promoting a religion - a "non-deity-based" secular humanism system of belief.

The U.S. Supreme Court, in *Abington Township v. Schempp* (1963), wrote:

> The state may not establish a "religion of secularism" in the sense of affirmatively opposing or showing hostility to religion, thus "preferring those who believe in no religion over those who do believe."...
>
> Refusal to permit religious exercises thus is seen, not as the realization of state neutrality, but rather as the establishment of a religion of secularism.[75]

The U.S. District Court, in *Crockett v.*

*Sorenson* (W.D. Va. 1983), wrote:

> The First Amendment was never intended to insulate our public institutions from any mention of God, the Bible or religion. When such insulation occurs, another religion, such as secular humanism, is effectively established.[76]

## BELIEF SYSTEM YOU VALUE MORE

The question is not whether a religion should or should not be in government, the question is whose religion - whose belief system - will be the basis for the government's actions.

The "non-deity-based" belief system has shown itself to be very intolerant, as when winning Nebraska football Coach Ron Brown was turned down for a coaching job at Stanford University because of his faith.

*The Daily Nebraskan,* April 13, 2002, reported:

> Pat Tetreault, co-chairwoman of the Committee of Gay, Lesbian, Bisexual and Transgender Concerns at University of Nebraska at Lincoln, stated "We shouldn't be discriminating on religion either, but you get into a slippery slope

on whose belief system you value more."[77]

## DEITY vs NON-DEITY BELIEF SYSTEMS

A nation's cannot be based on "deity" and "non-deity" at the same time, just as a car cannot be driving forward and reverse at the same time, or a light cannot be switched on and off at the same time. So the question is, which way is better?

America's founders thought belief in a Supreme Deity was better, as they acknowledged a Creator in the Declaration of Independence.

Benjamin Franklin wrote in *Maxims and Morals*:

> Freedom is not a gift bestowed upon us by other men, but a right that belongs to us by the laws of God.[78]

Samuel Adams wrote in *The Rights of the Colonists*, 1772:

> The right to freedom being the gift of God Almighty...may best be understood by reading and carefully studying the institutions of The Great Law Giver and the Head of the Christian Church.[79]

Thomas Jefferson wrote in N*otes on the State of Virginia*, 1781:

> God who gave us life gave us liberty. And can the liberties of a nation be thought secure when we have removed their only firm basis, a conviction in the minds of the people that these liberties are of the Gift of God?[80]

Alexander Hamilton stated:

> Natural liberty is a gift of the beneficent Creator, to the whole human race; and that civil liberty is founded in that; and cannot be wrested from any people, without the most manifest violation of justice.[81]

Thomas Paine wrote in *The American Crisis*, December 23, 1776:

> Heaven knows how to put a price upon its goods; and it would be strange indeed if so celestial an article as freedom should not be highly rated.[82]

President Harry S Truman stated in a letter to John L. Sullivan, 1949:

America is dedicated to the conviction that all people are entitled by the gift of God to equal rights and freedoms...

Our greatness is and will be measured by the degree of our recognition of this fundamental truth.[83]

The Supreme Court, *Zorach v Clauson,* 1952, said:

Our institutions presuppose a Supreme Being.[84]

Herbert Hoover remarked at a reception on his 80th birthday, 1954:

Our Founding Fathers did not invent the priceless boon of individual freedom and respect for the dignity of men.

That great gift to mankind sprang from the Creator and not from governments.[85]

Dwight Eisenhower stated February 20, 1955:

Without God, there could be no American form of Government,

nor an American way of life. Recognition of the Supreme Being is the first-the most basic-expression of Americanism.[86]

Ronald Reagan stated at the Presidential Medal of Freedom Ceremony, 1993:

> History comes and goes, but principles endure and insure future generations to defend liberty - not a gift from government, but a blessing from our Creator.[87]

President George W. Bush, in his State of the Union Address, January 28, 2003, stated:

> Liberty is not America's gift to the world, it is God's gift to humanity.[88]

# THREE SECULAR REASONS

America's founders had a "deity-based" belief system.

Why? Because:

1) Your RIGHTS cannot be taken away by the government if they come from a power "higher" than the government - i.e. Creator God;

2) There are no second class citizens if each person is EQUAL because each is made in the image of God;

3) You can live in freedom with few laws if the populous keeps internal laws because they are conscious of their ACCOUNTABILITY to God.

Government cannot be religion "neutral." It will always have thoughts underlying its actions. It will always have a belief system - a religion.

The choice is "whose belief system" will be the basis for the government's actions.

If the founder's "deity-based" belief system is removed, then the rights and freedoms based on that belief system are also removed.

In 1786, Dr. Benjamin Rush, signer of the Declaration of Independence and Treasurer of the U.S. Mint, wrote *Thoughts Upon the Mode of Education Proper in a Republic*, 1786:

I beg leave to remark that the only foundation for a useful education in a republic is to be laid on the foundation of religion.

Without this there can be no virtue, and without virtue there can be no liberty, and liberty is the object and life of all republican governments.

Such is my veneration for every religion that reveals the attributes of the Deity, or a future state of rewards and punishments, that I had rather see the opinions of Confucius or Mohamed inculcated upon our youth than to see them grow up wholly devoid of a system of religious principles.

But the religion I mean to recommend in this place is that of the New Testament.

It is not my purpose to hint at the arguements which establish the truth of the Christian revelation.

My only business is to declare that all its doctrines and precepts are calculated to promote the happiness of society and the safety and well-being of civil government.

A Christian cannot fail of being a republican...for every precept of the Gospel inculcates those degrees of humility, self-denial, and brotherly kindness which are directly opposed to the pride of monarchy....

A Christian cannot fail of being useful to the republic, for his religion teaches him that no man "liveth to himself."

And lastly a Christian cannot fail of being wholly inoffensive, for his religion teaches him in all things to do to others what he would wish, in like circumstances, they should do to him.[89]

President Calvin Coolidge, unveiling to the Equestrian Statue of Bishop Francis Asbury, Washington, D.C., October 15, 1924, stated:

Our government rests upon religion. It is from that source that we derive our reverence for truth and justice, for equality and liberty, and for the rights of mankind.

Unless the people believe in these principles they cannot believe in our government.[90]

Patrick Henry stated:

> Bad men cannot make good citizens. It is impossible that a nation of infidels or idolaters should be a nation of free-men.[91]

President Ronald Reagan, August 23, 1984, summed up the situation at a prayer breakfast in Reunion Arena, Dallas, Texas:

> Without God there is a coarsening of the society; without God democracy will not and cannot long endure....
> If we ever forget that we are One Nation Under God, then we will be a Nation gone under.[92]

# APPENDIX

All 50 States have at some point in their history acknowledged God in their STATE CONSTITUTIONS:

### Alabama 1901
Preamble:
"**W**e the people of the State of Alabama... invoking the favor and guidance of Almighty God, do ordain and establish the following Constitution..."[93]

### Alaska 1956
Preamble:
"**W**e, the people of Alaska, grateful to God and to those who founded our nation and pioneered this great land..."[94]

### Arizona 1911
Preamble:
"**W**e, the people of the State of Arizona, grateful to Almighty God for our liberties, do ordain this Constitution..."[95]

## Arkansas 1874
Preamble:

"We, the people of the State of Arkansas, grateful to Almighty God for the privilege of choosing our own form of government..."[96]

## California 1879
Preamble:

"We, the People of the State of California, grateful to Almighty God for our freedom..."[97]

## Colorado 1876
Preamble:

"We, the people of Colorado, with profound reverence for the Supreme Ruler of Universe..."[98]

## Connecticut 1818
Preamble

"The People of Connecticut, acknowledging with gratitude the good Providence of God in permitting them to enjoy..."[99]

## Delaware 1897
Preamble:

"Through Divine Goodness all men have, by nature, the rights of worshipping and serving their Creator according to the dictates of their consciences..."[100]

## Florida 1885

Preamble:

"We, the people of the State of Florida, grateful to Almighty God for our constitutional liberty...establish this Constitution..."[101]

## Georgia 1777

Preamble

"We, the people of Georgia, relying upon protection and guidance of Almighty God, do ordain and establish this Constitution..."[102]

## Hawaii 1959

Preamble:

"We, the people of Hawaii, Grateful for Divine Guidance...establish this Constitution..."[103]

## Idaho 1889

Preamble:

"We, the people of the State of Idaho, grateful to Almighty God for our freedom, to secure its blessings..."[104]

## Illinois 1870

Preamble:

"We, the people of the State of Illinois, grateful to Almighty God for the civil, political and religious liberty which He hath so long permitted us to enjoy and looking to Him for a blessing on our endeavors..."[105]

## Indiana 1851

Preamble:

"We, the People of the State of Indiana, grateful to Almighty God for the free exercise of the right to chose our form of government..."[106]

## Iowa 1857

Preamble:

"We, the People of the State of Iowa, grateful to the Supreme Being for the blessings hitherto enjoyed, and feeling our dependence on Him for a continuation of these blessings... establish this Constitution..."[107]

## Kansas 1859

Preamble:

"We, the people of Kansas, grateful to Almighty God for our civil and religious privileges...establish this Constitution..."[108]

## Kentucky 1891

Preamble:

"We, the people of the Commonwealth of Kentucky, grateful to Almighty God for the civil, political and religious liberties..."[109]

## Louisiana 1921

Preamble:

"We, the people of the State of Louisiana, grateful to Almighty God for the civil, political and religious liberties we enjoy...[110]

## Maine 1820

Preamble:

"We the People of Maine...acknowledging with grateful hearts the goodness of the Sovereign Ruler of the Universe in affording us an opportunity...and imploring His aid and direction..."[111]

## Maryland 1776

Preamble:

"We, the people of the state of Maryland, grateful to Almighty God for our civil and religious liberty..."[112]

## Massachusetts 1780

Preamble:

"We...the people of Massachusetts, acknowledging with grateful hearts, the goodness of the Great Legislator of the Universe...in the course of His Providence, an opportunity...and devoutly imploring His direction..."[113]

## Michigan 1908

Preamble:

"We, the people of the State of Michigan, grateful to Almighty God for the blessings of freedom...establish this Constitution..."[114]

## Minnesota 1857

Preamble:

"We, the people of the State of Minnesota, grateful to God for our civil and religious liberty, and desiring to perpetuate its blessings..."[115]

## Mississippi 1890

Preamble:

"We, the people of Mississippi in convention assembled, grateful to Almighty God, and invoking His blessing on our work..."[116]

## Missouri 1945

Preamble:

"We, the people of Missouri, with profound reverence for the Supreme Ruler of the Universe, and grateful for His goodness...establish this Constitution..."[117]

## Montana 1889

Preamble:

"We, the people of Montana, grateful to Almighty God for the blessings of liberty... establish this Constitution..."[118]

## Nebraska 1875

Preamble:

"We, the people, grateful to Almighty God for our freedom...establish this Constitution..."[119]

## Nevada 1864

Preamble:

"We the people of the State of Nevada, grateful to Almighty God for our freedom... establish this Constitution..."[120]

## New Hampshire 1792

Part I. Art. I. Sec. V:

"Every individual has a natural and unalienable right to worship God according to the dictates of his own conscience..."[121]

## New Jersey 1844

Preamble:

"We, the people of the State of New Jersey, grateful to Almighty God for civil and religious liberty which He hath so long permitted us to enjoy, and looking to Him for a blessing on our endeavors..."[122]

## New Mexico 1911

Preamble:

"We, the People of New Mexico, grateful to Almighty God for the blessings of liberty..."[123]

## New York 1846

Preamble:

"We, the people of the State of New York, grateful to Almighty God for our freedom, in order to secure its blessings..."[124]

## North Carolina 1868
Preamble:

"We the people of the State of North Carolina, grateful to Almighty God, the Sovereign Ruler of Nations, for...our civil, political, and religious liberties, and acknowledging our dependence upon Him for the continuance of those..."[125]

## North Dakota 1889
Preamble:

"We, the people of North Dakota, grateful to Almighty God for the blessings of civil and religious liberty, do ordain..."[126]

## Ohio 1852
Preamble:

"We the people of the state of Ohio, grateful to Almighty God for our freedom, to secure its blessings and to promote our common..."[127]

## Oklahoma 1907
Preamble:

"Invoking the guidance of Almighty God, in order to secure and perpetuate the blessings of liberty...establish this Constitution..."[128]

## Oregon 1857
Bill of Rights, Article I. Section 2:

"All men shall be secure in the Natural right, to worship Almighty God according to the dictates of their consciences..."[129]

## Pennsylvania 1776

Preamble:

"We, the people of Pennsylvania, grateful to Almighty God for the blessings of civil and religious liberty, and humbly invoking His guidance..."[130]

## Rhode Island 1842

Preamble:

"We the People of the State of Rhode Island...grateful to Almighty God for the civil and religious liberty which He hath so long permitted us to enjoy, and looking to Him for a blessing..."[131]

## South Carolina 1778

Preamble:

"We, the people of the State of South Carolina...grateful to God for our liberties, do ordain and establish this Constitution..."[132]

## South Dakota 1889

Preamble:

"We, the people of South Dakota, grateful to Almighty God for our civil and religious liberties...establish this Constitution..."[133]

## Tennessee 1796

Art. XI.III:

"That all men have a natural and indefeasible right to worship Almighty God according to the dictates of their conscience..."[134]

## Texas 1845
Preamble:

"We the People of the Republic of Texas, acknowledging, with gratitude, the grace and beneficence of God..."[135]

## Utah 1896
Preamble:

"Grateful to Almighty God for life and liberty, we...establish this Constitution..."[136]

## Vermont 1777
Preamble:

"Whereas all government ought to...enable the individuals who compose it to enjoy their natural rights, and other blessings which the Author of Existence has bestowed on man..."[137]

## Virginia 1776
Bill of Rights, XVI:

"Religion, or the Duty which we owe our Creator...can be directed only by Reason... and that it is the mutual duty of all to practice Christian Forbearance, Love and Charity towards each other..."[138]

## Washington 1889
Preamble:

"We the People of the State of Washington, grateful to the Supreme Ruler of the Universe for our liberties, do ordain this Constitution..."[139]

## West Virginia 1872

Preamble:

"Since through Divine Providence we enjoy the blessings of civil, political and religious liberty, we, the people of West Virginia...reaffirm our faith in and constant reliance upon God..."[140]

## Wisconsin 1848

Preamble:

"We, the people of Wisconsin, grateful to Almighty God for our freedom, domestic tranquility..."[141]

## Wyoming 1890

Preamble:

"We, the people of the State of Wyoming, grateful to God for our civil, political, and religious liberties...establish this Constitution..."[142]

# APPENDIX

## INAUGURAL ADDRESSES

Beginning with George Washington, the tradition has been for the President to be sworn into office with their hand upon a Bible and end their oath with the phrase "So help me, God."

Every past President has acknowledged God in their address upon assuming office:[143]

### 1st U.S. President
### GEORGE WASHINGTON
APRIL 30, 1789, FIRST INAUGURAL ADDRESS:

"It would be peculiarly improper to omit, in this first official act, my fervent supplications to that Almighty Being who rules over the universe, who presides in the councils of nations and whose providential aids can supply every human defect....

In tendering this homage to the Great Author of every public and private good, I assure myself that it expresses your sentiments not less than my own....

We ought to be no less persuaded that the propitious smiles of Heaven can never be expected on a nation that disregards the eternal rules of order and right which Heaven itself has ordained."

## 2nd U.S. President
## JOHN ADAMS

MARCH 4, 1797, INAUGURAL ADDRESS:

"With humble reverence, I feel it to be my duty to add, if a veneration for the religion of a people who profess and call themselves Christians, and a fixed resolution to consider a decent respect for Christianity among the best recommendations for the public service, can enable me in any degree to comply with your wishes, it shall be my strenuous endeavor that this sagacious injunction of the two Houses shall not be without effect....

May that Being who is supreme over all, the Patron of Order, the Fountain of Justice, and the Protector in all ages of the world of virtuous liberty, continue His blessings upon this nation."

## 3rd U.S. President
## THOMAS JEFFERSON

MARCH 4, 1801, FIRST INAUGURAL ADDRESS:

"Enlightened by a benign religion, professed, indeed, and practiced in various forms, yet all of them inculcating honesty, truth, temperance, gratitude, and the love of man; acknowledging and adoring an overruling Providence, which by all its dispensations proves that it delights in the happiness of man here and his greater happiness hereafter.

With all these blessings, what more is necessary to make us a happy and prosperous people?

Still one thing more...a wise and frugal Government, which shall restrain men from injuring one another, shall leave them otherwise free to regulate their own pursuits of industry and improvement, and shall not take from the mouth of labor the bread it has earned."

### 3rd U.S. President
### THOMAS JEFFERSON
MARCH 4, 1805, SECOND INAUGURAL
ADDRESS:

**"I** know that the acquisition of Louisiana has been disapproved by some from a candid apprehension that the enlargement of our territory would endanger the union, but who can limit the extent to which the federative principle may operate effectively?...

In matters of religion I have considered that its free exercise is placed by the Constitution independent of the powers of the General Government.

I have therefore undertaken, on no occasion, to prescribe the religious exercise suited to it; but have left them, as the Constitution found them, under the direction and discipline of state and church authorities by the several religious societies."

## 3rd U.S. President
## THOMAS JEFFERSON
MARCH 4, 1805, SECOND INAUGURAL
ADDRESS:

"I shall need, too, the favor of that Being in whose hands we are, who led our forefathers, as Israel of old, from their native land and planted them in a country flowing with all the necessities and comforts of life, who has covered our infancy with His Providence and our riper years with His wisdom and power, and to whose goodness I ask you to join with me in supplications that He will so enlighten the minds of your servants, guide their councils and prosper their measures, that whatever they do shall result in your good, and shall secure to you the peace, friendship and approbation of all nations."

## 4th U.S. President
## JAMES MADISON
MARCH 4, 1809, FIRST INAUGURAL ADDRESS:

"In these my confidence will under every difficulty be best placed, next to that which we have all been encouraged to feel in the guardianship and guidance of that Almighty Being whose power regulates the destiny of nations, whose blessings have been so conspicuously dispensed to this rising Republic, and to whom we are bound to address our devout gratitude for the past, as well as our fervent supplications and best hopes for the future."

## 4th U.S President
## JAMES MADISON
MARCH 4, 1813, SECOND INAUGURAL
ADDRESS:

"**I** should be compelled to shrink if I had less reliance on the support of an enlightened and generous people, and felt less deeply a conviction that the war with a powerful nation, which forms so prominent a feature in our situation, is stamped with that justice which invites the smiles of Heaven on the means of conducting it to a successful termination."

## 5th U.S. President
## JAMES MONROE
MARCH 4, 1817, FIRST INAUGURAL ADDRESS:

"**W**ho has been deprived of any right of person or property? Who restrained from offering his vows in the mode which he prefers to the Divine Author of his being?

It is well known that all these blessings have been enjoyed in their fullest....If we persevere... we can not fail, under the favor of a gracious Providence....

I enter on the trust to which I have been called by the suffrages of my fellow-citizens with my fervent prayers to the Almighty that He will be graciously pleased to continue to us that protection which He has already so conspicuously displayed."

## 5th U.S. President
## JAMES MONROE
MARCH 5, 1821, SECOND INAUGURAL
ADDRESS:

"That these powerful causes exist, and that they are permanent, is my fixed opinion; that they may produce a like accord in all questions touching, however remotely, the liberty, prosperity, and happiness of our country will always be the object of my most fervent prayers to the Supreme Author of All Good....

With full confidence in the continuance of that candor and generous indulgence from my fellow-citizens at large which I have heretofore experienced, and with a firm reliance on the protection of Almighty God, I shall forthwith commence the duties of the high trust to which you have called me."

## 6th U.S. President
## JOHN QUINCY ADAMS
MARCH 4, 1825, INAUGURAL ADDRESS.

"I appear, my fellow-citizens, in your presence and in that of Heaven to bind myself by the solemnities of religious obligation to the faithful performance of the duties allotted to me....

Freedom of the press and of religious opinion should be inviolate; the policy of our country is peace and the ark of our salvation union are articles of faith upon which we are all now agreed....and knowing that 'Except the Lord keep the city, the watchman waketh in vain,' with fervent supplications for His favor, to His overruling providence I commit with humble but fearless confidence my own fate and the future destinies of my country."

## 7th U.S. President
## ANDREW JACKSON
MARCH 4, 1829, FIRST INAUGURAL ADDRESS, LESS THAN THREE MONTHS AFTER HIS WIFE DIED:

"As long as our Government is administered for the good of the people, and is regulated by their will; as long as it secures to us the rights of person and of property, liberty of conscience and of the press, it will be worth defending....

And a firm reliance on the goodness of that Power whose providence mercifully protected our national infancy, and has since upheld our liberties in various vicissitudes, encourages me to offer up my ardent supplications that He will continue to make our beloved country the object of His divine care and gracious benediction."

## 7th U.S. President
## ANDREW JACKSON
MARCH 4, 1833, SECOND INAUGURAL ADDRESS:

"Finally, it is my fervent prayer to that Almighty Being before whom I now stand, and who has kept us in His hands from the infancy of our Republic to the present day...that He will so overrule all my intentions and actions and inspire the hearts of my fellow-citizens that we may be preserved from dangers of all kinds and continue forever a united happy people."

## 8th U.S. President
## MARTIN VAN BUREN
MARCH 4, 1837, INAUGURAL ADDRESS:

"So sensibly, fellow-citizens, do these circumstances press themselves upon me that I should not dare to enter upon my path of duty did I not look for the generous aid of those who will be associated with me in the various and coordinate branches of the Government; did I not repose with unwavering reliance on the patriotism, the intelligence, and the kindness of a people who never yet deserted a public servant honestly laboring in their cause; and above all, did I not permit myself humbly to hope for the sustaining of an ever-watchful and beneficent Providence."

## 8th U.S. President
## MARTIN VAN BUREN
MARCH 4, 1837, INAUGURAL ADDRESS:

"I only look to the gracious protection of that Divine Being whose strengthening support I humbly solicit, and whom I fervently pray to look down upon us all.

May it be among the dispensations of His Providence to bless our beloved country with honors and length of days; may her ways be pleasantness, and all her paths peace!"

## 9th U.S. President
## WILLIAM HENRY HARRISON

MARCH 4, 1841, INAUGURAL ADDRESS, DELIVERED ONLY 30 DAYS BEFORE HIS DEATH:

"**I** too well understand the dangerous temptations to which I shall be exposed from the magnitude of the power which it has been the pleasure of the people to commit to my hands not to place my chief confidence upon the aid of that Almighty Power which has hitherto protected me and enabled me....

We admit of no government by divine right, believing that so far as power is concerned the Beneficent Creator has made no distinction amongst men; that all are upon an equality, and that the only legitimate right to govern is an express grant of power from the governed."

## 9th U.S. President
## WILLIAM HENRY HARRISON

MARCH 4, 1841, INAUGURAL ADDRESS:

"**T**he maxim which our ancestors derived from the mother country that 'freedom of the press is the great bulwark of civil and religious liberty' is one of the most precious legacies which they have left us."

## 9th U.S. President
## WILLIAM HENRY HARRISON

MARCH 4, 1841, INAUGURAL ADDRESS:

"Limited as are the powers which have been granted, still enough have been granted to constitute a despotism if concentrated in one of the departments....

The tendency of power to increase itself, particularly when exercised by a single individual... would terminate in virtual monarchy....

As long as the love of power is a dominant passion of the human bosom, and as long as the understanding of men can be warped and their affections changed by operations upon their passions and prejudices, so long will the liberties of a people depend on their constant attention to its preservation....

The tendencies of all such governments in their decline is to monarchy, and the antagonist principle to liberty there is the spirit of faction - a spirit which assumes the character and in times of great excitement imposes itself upon the people as the genuine spirit of freedom, and, like the false christs whose coming was foretold by the Savior, seeks to, and were it possible would, impose upon the true and most faithful disciples of liberty.

It is in periods like this that it behooves the people to be most watchful of those to whom they have intrusted power."

## 9th U.S. President
## WILLIAM HENRY HARRISON
MARCH 4, 1841, INAUGURAL ADDRESS:

"**I** deem the present occasion sufficiently important and solemn to justify me in expressing to my fellow citizens a profound reverence for the Christian religion, and a thorough conviction that sound morals, religious liberty, and a just sense of religious responsibility are essentially connected with all true and lasting happiness;

And to that good Being who has blessed us by the gifts of civil and religious freedom, who watched over and prospered the labors of our fathers and has hitherto preserved to us institutions far exceeding in excellence those of any other people, let us unite in fervently commending every interest of our beloved country in all future time."

## 10th U.S. President
## JOHN TYLER
APRIL 9, 1841, ADDRESS DELIVERED UPON ASSUMING THE PRESIDENCY AFTER THE DEATH OF PRESIDENT HARRISON:

"**F**or the first time in our history the person elected to the Vice-Presidency...has had devolved upon him the Presidential office....

My earnest prayer shall be constantly addressed to the all-wise and all-powerful Being who made me, and by whose dispensation I am called to the high office of President....

Confiding in the protecting care of an everwatchful and overruling Providence, it shall be my first and highest duty to preserve unimpaired the free institutions under which we live and transmit them to those who shall succeed me in their full force and vigor."

## 10th U.S. President
## JOHN TYLER
APRIL 13, 1841, PROCLAMATION OF A
NATIONAL DAY OF FASTING AND PRAYER
UPON THE DEATH OF PRESIDENT HARRISON:

"When a Christian people feel themselves to be overtaken by a great public calamity, it becomes them to humble themselves under the dispensation of Divine Providence, to recognize His righteous government over the children of men, to acknowledge His goodness in time past, as well as their own unworthiness, and to supplicate His merciful protection for the future....to impress all minds with a sense of the uncertainty of human things and of the dependence of nations, as well as individuals, upon our Heavenly Parent."

## 10th U.S. President
## JOHN TYLER
APRIL 13, 1841, IN A PROCLAMATION OF A
NATIONAL DAY OF FASTING AND PRAYER
UPON THE DEATH OF WILLIAM HENRY
HARRISON, WASHINGTON, D.C:

"We may all with one accord join in

humble and reverential approach to Him in whose hands we are, invoking Him to inspire us with a proper spirit and temper of heart and mind under these frowns of His providence and still to bestow His gracious benedictions upon our Government and our country."

## 11th U.S. President
## JAMES KNOX POLK
MARCH 4, 1845, INAUGURAL ADDRESS:

"**I** fervently invoke the aid of that Almighty Ruler of the Universe in whose hands are the destinies of nations and of men to guard this Heaven-favored land....

The Republic of Texas has made known her desire to come into our Union, to form a part of our Confederacy and enjoy with us the blessings of liberty secured and guaranteed by our Constitution....

I enter upon the discharge of the high duties which have been assigned to me by the people, again humbly supplicating that Divine Being, who has watched over and protected our beloved country from its infancy to the present hour."

## 12th U.S. President
## ZACHARY TAYLOR
MARCH 5, 1849, INAUGURAL ADDRESS, DELIVERED A DAY LATER THAN USUAL AS HE REFUSED TO BE SWORN IN ON SUNDAY IN HONOR OF THE SABBATH:

"Our geographical position, the genius of our institutions and our people, the advancing spirit of civilization, and, above all, the dictates of religion direct us to the cultivation of peaceful and friendly relations with all other powers....

In conclusion I congratulate you, my fellow-citizens, upon the high state of prosperity to which the goodness of Divine Providence has conducted our common country. Let us invoke a continuance of the same protecting care which has led us from small beginnings to the eminence we this day occupy."

## 13th U.S. President
## MILLARD FILLMORE
JULY 10, 1850, ADDRESS TO CONGRESS, DELIVERED UPON ASSUMING THE PRESIDENCY AFTER THE DEATH OF PRESIDENT TAYLOR:

"A great man has fallen among us, and a whole country is called to an occasion of unexpected, deep, and general mourning....

I appeal to you to aid me, under the trying circumstances which surround me, in the discharge of the duties from which, however much I may be oppressed by them, I dare not shrink; and I rely upon Him who holds in His hands the destinies of nations to endow me with the requisite strength for the task and to avert from our country the evils apprehended from the heavy calamity which has befallen us."

## 14th U.S. President
## FRANKLIN PIERCE

MARCH 4, 1853, INAUGURAL ADDRESS, ONLY
TWO MONTHS AFTER HIS ELEVEN YEAR
ONLY SON, BENNIE, WAS KILLED AS THEIR
CAMPAIGN TRAIN ROLLED OFF THE TRACKS:

**"O**ur fathers decided for themselves, both upon the hour to declare and the hour to strike.

They were their own judges of the circumstances under which it became them to pledge to each other 'their lives, their fortunes, and their sacred honor' for the acquisition of the priceless inheritance transmitted to us.

The energy with which that great conflict was opened was under the guidance of a manifest and beneficent Providence."

## 14th U.S. President
## FRANKLIN PIERCE

MARCH 4, 1853, INAUGURAL ADDRESS:

**"T**he dangers of a concentration of all power in the General government of a confederacy so vast as ours are too obvious to be disregarded. You have a right...to expect your agents in every department to regard strictly the limits imposed upon them by the Constitution....

Liberty rests upon a proper distribution of power between the State and Federal authorities....

With the Union my best and dearest earthly hopes are entwined. Without it what are we individually or collectively?

What becomes of the noblest field ever opened for the advancement of our race in religion, in government, in the arts, and in all that dignifies and adorns mankind."

## 14th U.S. President
## FRANKLIN PIERCE
MARCH 4, 1853, INAUGURAL ADDRESS:

"It is with me an earnest and vital belief that as the Union has been the source, under Providence, of our prosperity to this time, so it is the surest pledge of a continuance of the blessings we have enjoyed, and which we are sacredly bound to transmit undiminished to our children....

But let not the foundation of our hope rest upon man's wisdom....It must be felt that there is no national security but in the nation's humble, acknowledged dependence upon God and His overruling providence....

With all the cherished memories of the past gathering around me like so many eloquent voices of exhortation from Heaven, I can express no better hope for my country than that the kind Providence which smiled upon our fathers may enable their children to preserve the blessings they have inherited."

## 15th U.S. President
## JAMES BUCHANAN
MARCH 4, 1857, INAUGURAL ADDRESS:

"In entering upon this great office I must

humbly invoke the God of our fathers for wisdom and firmness to execute its high and responsible duties....

We should never forget....those exiles from foreign shores who may seek in this country to improve their condition and to enjoy the blessings of civil and religious liberty....

We ought to cultivate peace, commerce, and friendship with all nations, and this not merely as the best means of promoting our own material interests, but in a spirit of Christian benevolence toward our fellow-men, wherever their lot may be cast...

In all our acquisitions the people, under the protection of the American flag, have enjoyed civil and religious liberty....

I shall now proceed to take the oath prescribed by the Constitution, whilst humbly invoking the blessing of Divine Providence on this great people."

## 16th U.S. President
## ABRAHAM LINCOLN
MARCH 4, 1861, FIRST INAUGURAL ADDRESS:
"The candid citizen must confess that if the policy of the Government upon vital questions affecting the whole people is to be irrevocably fixed by decisions of the Supreme Court, the instant they are made...the people will have ceased to be their own rulers, having to that extent practically resigned their Government into the

hands of the eminent tribunal....

Intelligence, patriotism, Christianity, and a firm reliance on Him who has never yet forsaken this favored land, are still competent to adjust in the best way all our present difficulty."

## 16th U.S. President
## ABRAHAM LINCOLN

MARCH 4, 1865, SECOND INAUGURAL ADDRESS, 45 DAYS BEFORE HIS ASSASSINATION:

"Both read the same Bible and pray to the same God....The prayers of both could not be answered. That of neither has been answered fully. The Almighty has His own purposes. 'Woe unto the world because of offenses'...

Yet, if God will that it continue until all the wealth piled by the bondsmen's two hundred and fifty years of unrequited toil shall be sunk, and until every drop of blood drawn with the lash shall be paid by another drawn with the sword, as was said three thousand years ago, so still it must be said 'the Judgements of the Lord are true and righteous altogether.'"

## 17th U.S. President
## ANDREW JOHNSON

APRIL 15, 1865, ADDRESS UPON ASSUMING THE PRESIDENCY FOLLOWING THE ASSASSINATION OF PRESIDENT LINCOLN:

"Duties have been mine; consequences are God's."

# 17th U.S. President
## ANDREW JOHNSON
APRIL 25, 1865, PROCLAMATION OF A
NATIONAL DAY OF HUMILIATION & MOURNING
UPON ASSUMING PRESIDENCY:

"**W**hereas our country has become one great house of mourning, where the head of the family has been taken away, and believing that a special period should be assigned for again humbling ourselves before Almighty God,...

Now, therefore, in order to mitigate that grief on earth which can only be assuaged by communion with the Father in Heaven...I recommend my fellow-citizens then to assemble in their respective places of worship, there to unite in solemn service to Almighty God in memory of the good man who has been removed."

## 17th U.S. President
ANDREW JOHNSON, APRIL 29, 1865,
RECOMMENDATIONS REGARDING THE
PROCLAMATION OF A NATIONAL DAY OF
HUMILIATION AND PRAYER:

"**M**y proclamation of the 25th instant Thursday, the 25th day of next month, was recommended as a day for special humiliation and prayer in consequence of the assassination of Abraham Lincoln...

But whereas my attention has since been called to the fact that the day aforesaid is sacred to large numbers of Christians as one of rejoicing for the ascension of the Savior:

Now, therefore, be it known that I, Andrew Johnson, President of the United States, do hereby suggest that the religious services recommended as aforesaid should be postponed until Thursday, the 1st day of June next."

## 18th U.S. President
## ULYSSES SIMPSON GRANT
MARCH 4, 1869, FIRST INAUGURAL ADDRESS:

"In conclusion I ask patient forbearance one toward another throughout the land, and a determined effort on the part of every citizen to do his share toward cementing a happy union; and I ask the prayers of the nation to Almighty God in behalf of this consummation."

## 18th U.S. President
## ULYSSES SIMPSON GRANT
MARCH 4, 1873, SECOND INAUGURAL ADDRESS:

"Under Providence, I have been called a second time to act as Executive over this great nation...I do believe that our Great Maker is preparing the world, in His own good time, to become one nation, speaking one language, and then armies and navies will no longer be required."

## 19th U.S. President
## RUTHERFORD BIRCHARD HAYES
MARCH 5, 1877, INAUGURAL ADDRESS,
DELIVERED A DAY LATER THAN USUAl as
he REFUSed TO BE SWORN IN on SUNDAY IN
HONOR OF THE SABBATH. HE took THE OATH
with HIS PALM PLACED ON PSALM 118:13 &
KISSED THE BIBLE:

"Looking for the guidance of that Divine Hand by which the destinies of nations and individuals are shaped, I call upon you, Senators, Representatives, judges, fellow-citizens, here and everywhere, to unite with me in an earnest effort to secure to our country the blessings, not only of material property, but of justice, peace, and union."

## 20th U.S. President
## JAMES ABRAM GARFIELD
MARCH 4, 1881, INAUGURAL ADDRESS:

"Let our people find a new meaning in the divine oracle which declares that 'a little child shall lead them,' for our own little children will soon control the destinies of the Republic.

My countrymen, we do not now differ in our judgement concerning the controversies of past generations, and fifty years hence our children will not be divided in their opinions concerning our controversies.

They will surely bless their fathers and their fathers' God that the Union was preserved, that slavery was overthrown, and that both races were made equal before the law."

## 20th U.S. President
## JAMES ABRAM GARFIELD

MARCH 4, 1881, INAUGURAL ADDRESS:

"Before continuing the onward march let us pause on this height for a moment to strengthen our faith and renew our hope....

The emancipated race has already made remarkable progress. With unquestioning devotion to the Union, with a patience and gentleness not born of fear, they have 'followed the light as God gave them to see the light.'...

Above all, upon our efforts to promote the welfare of this great people and their Government I reverently invoke the support and blessings of Almighty God."

## 21st U.S. President
## CHESTER ALAN ARTHUR

SEPTEMBER 22, 1881, ADDRESS UPON ASSUMING THE PRESIDENCY AFTER PRESIDENT GARFIELD'S DEATH:

"For the fourth time in the history of the Republic its Chief Magistrate has been removed by death.

All hearts are filled with grief and horror at the hideous crime which has darkened our land, and the memory of the murdered President....

Summoned to these high duties and responsibilities and profoundly conscious of their magnitude and gravity, I assume the trust imposed by the Constitution, relying for aid on

Divine Guidance and the virtue, patriotism, and intelligence of the American people."

## 21st U.S. President
## CHESTER ALAN ARTHUR
SEPTEMBER 22, 1881, PROCLAMATION OF A NATIONAL DAY OF HUMILIATION & MOURNING UPON ASSUMING THE PRESIDENCY AFTER THE DEATH OF PRESIDENT GARFIELD:

"**W**hereas in His inscrutable wisdom it has pleased God to remove from us the illustrious head of the nation, James A. Garfield, late President of the United States; and

Whereas It is fitting that the deep grief which fills all hearts should manifest itself with one accord toward the Throne of Infinite Grace, and that we should bow before the Almighty and seek from Him that consolation in our affliction and that sanctification of our loss which He is able and willing to vouchsafe:

Now, therefore, in obedience to sacred duty and in accordance with the desire of the people, I, Chester A. Arthur, President of the United States of America, do hereby appoint Monday next, the 26th day of September – on which day the remains of our honored and beloved dead will be consigned to their last resting place on earth - to be observed throughout the United States as a day of humiliation and mourning;

And I earnestly recommend all the people to assemble on that day in their respective places of divine worship, there to render alike their tribute of sorrowful submission to the will of Almighty God and of reverence and love for the memory and character of our late Chief Magistrate."

## 22nd U.S. President
## (STEPHEN) GROVER CLEVELAND

MARCH 4, 1885, FIRST INAUGURAL ADDRESS:

"On this auspicious occasion we may well renew the pledge of our devotion to the Constitution, which, launched by the founders of the Republic and consecrated by their prayers and patriotic devotion, has for almost a century borne the hopes and the aspirations of a great people....

And let us not trust to human effort alone, but humbly acknowledge the power and goodness of Almighty God who presides over the destiny of nations, and who has at all times been revealed in our country's history, let us invoke His aid and His blessings upon our labors."

## 23rd U.S. President
## BENJAMIN HARRISON

MARCH 4, 1889, INAUGURAL ADDRESS:

"Entering thus solemnly into covenant with each other, we may reverently invoke and confidently extend the favor and help of Almighty God - that He will give to me wisdom, strength, and fidelity, and to our people a spirit of fraternity and a love of righteousness and peace....

God has placed upon our head a diadem

and has laid at our feet power and wealth beyond definition or calculation.

But we must not forget that we take these gifts upon the condition that justice and mercy shall hold the reins of power and the upward avenues of hope shall be free to all people."

## 24th U.S. President
## (STEPHEN) GROVER CLEVELAND

MARCH 4, 1893, SECOND INAUGURAL ADDRESS:

"My Fellow-Citizens: In obedience to the mandate of my countrymen I am about to dedicate myself to their service under the sanction of a solemn oath.

Deeply moved by the expression of confidence and personal attachment which has called me to this service, I am sure my gratitude can make no better return than the pledge I now give before God and these witnesses of unreserved and complete devotion to the interests and welfare of those who have honored me....

It can not be doubted that our stupendous achievements as a people and our country's robust strength have given rise to heedlessness of those laws governing our national health which we can no more evade than human life can escape the laws of God and nature....

Above all, I know there is a Supreme Being who rules the affairs of men and whose goodness and mercy have always followed the American people, and I know He will not turn from us now if we humbly and reverently seek His powerful aid."

## 25th U.S. President
## WILLIAM MCKINLEY

MARCH 4, 1897, FIRST INAUGURAL ADDRESS:

"**I** assume the arduous and responsible duties of President of the United States, relying upon the support of my countrymen and invoking the guidance of Almighty God.

Our faith teaches that there is no safer reliance than upon the God of our fathers, who has so singularly favored the American people in every national trial, and who will not forsake us so long as we obey His commandments and walk humbly in His footsteps....

It is consoling and encouraging to realize that free speech, a free press, free thought, free schools, the free and unmolested right of religious liberty and worship, and free and fair elections are dearer and more universally enjoyed to-day than ever before....

Illiteracy must be banished from the land if we shall attain that high destiny as the foremost of the enlightened nations of the world which, under Providence, we ought to achieve....

Let me again repeat the words of the oath administered by the Chief Justice which, in their respective spheres, so far as applicable, I would have all my countrymen observe:

'I will faithfully execute the office of the

President of the United States, and will, to the best of my ability, preserve, protect, and defend the Constitution of the United States.'

This is the obligation I have reverently taken before the Lord Most High. To keep it will be my single purpose, my constant prayer."

## 25th U.S. President
## WILLIAM MCKINLEY

MARCH 4, 1901, SECOND INAUGURAL ADDRESS:

"**I** enter upon its administration appreciating the great responsibilities which attach to this renewed honor and commission, promising unreserved devotion on my part to their faithful discharge and reverently invoking for my guidance the direction and favor of Almighty God.

'Hope maketh not ashamed.' The prophets of evil were not the builders of the Republic, nor in its crises since have they saved or served it.

The faith of the fathers was a mighty force in its creation, and the faith of their descendants has wrought its progress and furnished its defenders....

As hereunto, so hereafter will the nation demonstrate its fitness to administer any new estate which events devolve upon it, and in the fear of God will 'take occasion by the hand and make the bounds of freedom wider yet.'"

## 26th U.S. President
## THEODORE ROOSEVELT
SEPTEMBER 14, 1901, PROCLAMATION OF A
NATIONAL DAY OF MOURNING AND PRAYER,
ISSUED UPON ASSUMING THE PRESIDENCY
AFTER THE DEATH OF PRESIDENT MCKINLEY:

**"A** terrible bereavement has befallen our people. The President of the United States has been struck down; a crime not only against the Chief Magistrate, but against every law-abiding and liberty-loving citizen.

President McKinley crowned a life of largest love for his fellow men, of earnest endeavor for their welfare, by a death of Christian fortitude; and both the way in which he lived his life and the way in which, in the supreme hour of trial, he met death will remain forever a precious heritage of our people…

Now, therefore, I, Theodore Roosevelt, President of the United States of America, do appoint Thursday next, September 19, the day in which the body of the dead President will be laid in its last earthly resting place, as a day of mourning and prayer throughout the United States.

I earnestly recommend all the people to assemble on that day in their respective places of divine worship, there to bow down in submission to the will of Almighty God, and to pay out of full hearts the homage of love and reverence to the memory of the great and good President, whose death has so sorely smitten the nation."

## 26th U.S. President
## THEODORE ROOSEVELT
MARCH 4, 1905, INAUGURAL ADDRESS:

"No people on earth have more cause to be thankful than ours, and this is said reverently, in no spirit of boastfulness in our own strength, but with gratitude to the Giver of Good who has blessed us....

We wish peace, but we wish the peace of justice, the peace of righteousness....

If we fail, the cause of free self-government throughout the world will rock to its foundations, and therefore our responsibility is heavy, to ourselves, to the world as it is today, and to the generations yet unborn."

## 27th U.S. President
## WILLIAM HOWARD TAFT
MARCH 4, 1909, INAUGURAL ADDRESS:

"I invoke the considerate sympathy and support of my fellow-citizens and the aid of the Almighty God in the discharge of my responsible duties."

## 28th U.S. President
## (THOMAS) WOODROW WILSON
MARCH 4, 1913, FIRST INAUGURAL ADDRESS:

"The feelings with which we face this new age of right and opportunity sweep across our heartstrings like some air out of God's own presence, where justice and mercy are reconciled and the judge and the brother are one....

This is not a day of triumph; it is a day of dedication....

Men's hearts wait upon us; men's lives hang in the balance; men's hopes call upon us to day what we will do.

Who shall live up to the great trust? Who dare fail to try? I summon all honest men, all patriotic, all forward-looking men to my side. God helping me, I will not fail them."

## 28th U.S. President
## (THOMAS) WOODROW WILSON
MARCH 5, 1917, SECOND INAUGURAL ADDRESS:

"We are being forged into a new unity amidst the fires that now blaze throughout the world.

In their ardent heat we shall, in God's Providence, let us hope, be purged of faction and division, purified of the errant humors of party and of private interest, and shall stand forth in the days to come with a new dignity of national pride and spirit....

I know now what the task means. I realize to the full the responsibility which it involves. I pray God I may be given the wisdom and the prudence to do my duty in the true spirit of this great people"

# 29th U.S. President
## WARREN GAMALIEL HARDING

MARCH 4, 1921, INAUGURAL ADDRESS:

"Standing in this presence, mindful of the solemnity of this occasion, feeling the emotions which no one may know until he senses the great weight of responsibility for himself, I must utter my belief in the Divine Inspiration of the founding fathers.

Surely there must have been God's intent in the making of this new world Republic....

Let us express renewed and strengthened devotion, in grateful reverence for the immortal beginning, and utter our confidence in the supreme fulfillment.....

America is ready to encourage, eager to initiate, anxious to participate in any seemly program likely to lessen the probability of war, and promote that brotherhood of mankind which must be God's highest conception of human relationship....

My most reverent prayer for America is for industrial peace, with its rewards, widely and generally distributed, amid the inspirations of equal opportunity....

We want an America of homes, illumined with hope and happiness, where mothers, freed from the necessity for long hours of toil beyond their own doors, may preside as befits the hearthstone of American citizenship.

We want the cradle of American childhood

rocked under conditions so wholesome and so hopeful that no blight may touch it....

I would rejoice to acclaim the era of the Golden Rule."

## 29th U.S. President
## WARREN GAMALIEL HARDING
MARCH 4, 1921, INAUGURAL ADDRESS:

"One cannot stand in this presence and be unmindful of the tremendous responsibility. The world upheaval has added heavily to our tasks.

But with the realization comes the surge of high resolve, and there is reassurance in belief in the God given destiny of our Republic. If I felt that there is to be sole responsibility in the Executive for the America of tomorrow I should shrink from the burden.

But here are a hundred millions, with common concern and shared responsibility, answerable to God and country. The Republic summons them to their duty, and I invite cooperation.

I accept my part with single-mindedness of purpose and humility of spirit, and implore the favor and guidance of God in His Heaven. With these I am unafraid, and confidently face the future. I have taken the solemn oath of office on that passage of Holy Writ wherein it is asked:

'What doth the Lord require of thee but to do justly, and to love mercy, and to walk humbly with thy God.' This I plight to God and country."

## 30th U.S. President
## (JOHN) CALVIN COOLIDGE

AUGUST 4, 1923, PROCLAMATION OF A
NATIONAL DAY OF MOURNING AND PRAYER:

"In the inscrutable wisdom of Divine Providence, Warren Gamaliel Harding, twenty-ninth President of the United States, has been taken from us. The nation has lost a wise and enlightened statesman....

Now, therefore, I, Calvin Coolidge, President of the United States, do appoint Friday next, August tenth, the day on which the body of the dead President will be laid to its last earthly resting place, as a day of mourning and prayer throughout the United States.

I earnestly recommend the people to assemble on that day in their respective places of divine worship, there to bow down in submission to the will of Almighty God, and to pay out of full hearts the homage of love and reverence to the memory of the great and good President whose death has so sorely smitten the nation."

## 30th U.S. President
## (JOHN) CALVIN COOLIDGE

MARCH 4, 1925, INAUGURAL ADDRESS:

"If we wish to continue to be distinctly American, we must continue to make that term comprehensive enough to embrace the legitimate desires of a civilized and enlightened people determined in all their relations to pursue a conscientious and religious life....

Peace will come when there is realization that only under a reign of law, based on righteousness and supported by the religious conviction of the brotherhood of man, can there be any hope of a complete and satisfying life. Parchment will fail, the sword will fail, it is only the spiritual nature of man that can be triumphant....

America seeks no earthly empires built on blood and force. No ambition, no temptation, lures her to thought of foreign dominions.

The legions which she sends forth are armed, not with the sword, but with the Cross.

The higher state to which she seeks the allegiance of all mankind is not of human, but Divine origin. She cherishes no purpose save to merit the favor of Almighty God."

## 31st U.S. President
## HERBERT CLARK HOOVER
MARCH 4, 1929, INAUGURAL ADDRESS:

"This occasion is not alone the administration of the most sacred oath which can be assumed by an American citizen.

It is a dedication and consecration under God to the highest office in service of our people.

I assume this trust in the humility of knowledge that only through the guidance of Almighty Providence can I hope to discharge its ever-increasing burdens....

Knowing what the task means and the

responsibility which it involves, I beg your tolerance, your aid, and your cooperation.

I ask the help of Almighty God in this service to my country to which you have called me."

## 32nd U.S. President
## FRANKLIN DELANO ROOSEVELT
### MARCH 4, 1933, FIRST INAUGURAL ADDRESS:

"First of all, let me assert my firm belief that the only thing we have to fear is fear itself....

In such a spirit on my part and on yours we face our common difficulties. They concern, thank God, only material things....

Practices of the unscrupulous money changers stand indicted in the court of public opinion, rejected by the hearts and minds of men...

They know only the rules of a generation of self-seekers. They have no vision, and where there is no vision the people perish.(Pr. 29:18)

The money changers have fled from their high seats in the temple of our civilization. We may now restore that temple to the ancient truths....

We face arduous days that lie before us in the warm courage of national unity; with the clear consciousness of seeking old and precious moral values.... In this dedication of a nation we humbly ask the blessing of God. May He protect each and every one of us! May He guide me in the days to come."

## 32nd U.S. President
## FRANKLIN DELANO ROOSEVELT
JANUARY 20, 1937, SECOND INAUGURAL
ADDRESS:

"While this duty rests upon me I shall do my utmost to speak their purpose and to do their will, seeking Divine Guidance to help each and every one to give light to them that sit in darkness and to guide our feet into the way of peace."

## 32nd U.S. President
## FRANKLIN DELANO ROOSEVELT
JANUARY 20, 1941, THIRD INAUGURAL
ADDRESS:

"A nation, like a person, has something deeper, something more permanent, something larger than the sum of all its parts.

It is that something which matters most to its future - which calls forth the most sacred guarding of its present. It is a thing for which we find it difficult - even impossible - to hit upon a single, simple word.

And yet we all understand what it is - the spirit - the faith of America. It is the product of centuries. It was born in the multitudes of those who came from many lands - some of high degree, but mostly plain people, who sought here, early and late, to find freedom more freely.

The democratic aspiration is no mere recent phase of human history. It is human history. It permeated the ancient life of early peoples. It blazed anew in the middle ages.

It was written in the Magna Carta. In the Americas its impact has been irresistible.

America has been the New World in all tongues, to all peoples, not because this continent was a new-found land, but because all those who came here believed they could create upon this continent a new life - a life that should be new in freedom.

Its vitality was written into our own Mayflower Compact, into the Declaration of Independence, into the Constitution of the United States, into the Gettysburg Address....

If the spirit of America were killed, even though the Nation's body and mind, constricted in an alien world, lived on, the America we know would have perished. That spirit - that faith - speaks to us in our daily lives in ways often unnoticed....

We do not retreat. We are not content to stand still. As Americans, we go forward in the service of our country by the will of God."

## 32nd U.S. President
## FRANKLIN DELANO ROOSEVELT
JANUARY 20, 1945, FOURTH INAUGURAL
ADDRESS:

"As I stand here today, having taken the solemn oath of office in the presence of my fellow countrymen – in the presence of God - I know that it is America's purpose that we shall not fail....

The Almighty God has blessed our land in many ways. He has given our people stout hearts and strong arms with which to strike mighty blows for freedom and truth.

He has given to our country a faith which has become the hope of all peoples in an anguished world.

So we pray to Him now for the vision to see our way clearly - to see the way that leads to a better life for ourselves and for all our fellow men - to the achievement of His will, to peace on earth. In the presence of God - I know that it is America's purpose that we shall not fail."

## 33rd U.S. President
## HARRY S TRUMAN

APRIL 12, 1945, FIRST ADDRESS TO CONGRESS, DELIVERED UPON ASSUMING THE PRESIDENCY AFTER THE DEATH OF PRESIDENT ROOSEVELT:

"At this moment I have in my heart a prayer. As I have assumed my heavy duties, I humbly pray to Almighty God in the words of King Solomon:

'Give therefore Thy servant an understanding heart to judge Thy people that I may discern between good and bad; for who is able to judge this Thy so great a people?' I ask only to be a good and faithful servant of my Lord and my people."

# 33rd U.S. President
# HARRY S TRUMAN

JANUARY 20, 1949, INAUGURAL ADDRESS:

"In performing the duties of my office, I need the help and the prayers of every one of you....

The American people stand firm in the faith which has inspired this Nation from the beginning. We believe that all men have a right to equal justice under the law and equal opportunity to share in the common good. We believe that all men have the right to freedom of thought and expression.

We believe that all men are created equal because they are created in the image of God. From this faith we will not be moved....

Communism is based on the belief that man is so weak and inadequate that he is unable to govern himself, and therefore requires the rule of strong masters.

Democracy is based on the conviction that man has the moral and intellectual capacity, as well as the inalienable right, to govern himself with reason and justice.

Communism subjects the individual to arrest without lawful cause, punishment without trial, and forced labor as a chattel of the state. It decrees what information he shall receive, what art he shall produce, what leaders he shall follow, and what thoughts he shall think.

Democracy maintains that government is

established for the benefit of the individual, and is charged with the responsibility of protecting the rights of the individual and his freedom in the exercise of his abilities....

These differences between communism and democracy do not concern the United States alone.

People everywhere are coming to realize that what is involved is material well-being, human dignity, and the right to believe in and worship God....

We are aided by all who desire freedom of speech, freedom of religion, and freedom to live their own lives for useful ends. Our allies are the millions who hunger and thirst after righteousness (Mat. 5:6)....

Steadfast in our faith in the Almighty, we will advance toward a world, where man's freedom is secure. To that end we will devote our strength, our resources, and our firmness of resolve.

With God's help the future of mankind will be assured in a world of justice, harmony, and peace. I need the help and the prayers of every one of you."

## 34th U.S. President
## DWIGHT DAVID EISENHOWER
JANUARY 20, 1953, INAUGURAL ADDRESS, THE FIRST SUCH ADDRESS TO BE TELEVISED:

"**My** friends, before I begin the expression

of those thoughts that I deem appropriate to this moment, would you permit me the privilege of uttering a little private prayer of my own.

And I ask that you bow your heads. Almighty God, as we stand here at this moment, my future associates in the Executive Branch of our Government join me in beseeching that Thou will make full and complete our dedication to the service of the people in this throng and their fellow citizens everywhere.

Give us, we pray, the power to discern clearly right from wrong and allow all our words and actions to be governed thereby and by the laws of the land.

Especially we pray that our concern shall be for all the people regardless of station, race, or calling.

May cooperation be permitted and be the mutual aim of those who, under the concepts of our Constitution, hold to differing political faiths; so that all may work for the good of our beloved country and Thy glory. Amen."

### 34th U.S. President
### DWIGHT DAVID EISENHOWER
JANUARY 20, 1953, INAUGURAL ADDRESS, THE FIRST SUCH ADDRESS TO BE TELEVISED:

"**M**y fellow citizens....We are summoned by this honored and historic ceremony to witness more than the act of one citizen swearing his oath of service, in the presence of God.

We are called as a people to give testimony in the sight of the world our faith that the future shall belong to the free....In the swift rush of great events, we find ourselves groping to know the full sense and meaning of these times in which we live. In our quest of understanding, we beseech God's guidance....

At such a time in history, we who are free must proclaim anew our faith. This faith in America is the abiding creed of our fathers. It is our faith in the deathless dignity of man, governed by eternal moral and natural laws.

This faith defines our full view of life. It establishes beyond debate, those gifts of the Creator that are man's inalienable rights, and that makes all men equal in His sight....

This faith rules our whole way of life. It decrees that we, the people, elect leaders not to rule but to serve....

It is because we, all of us, hold to these principles that the political changes accomplished this day do not imply turbulence, upheaval or disorder.

Rather this change expresses a purpose of strengthening our dedication and devotion to the precepts of our founding documents, a conscious renewal of faith in our country and in the watchfulness of a Divine Providence.

The enemies of this faith know no god but force, no devotion but it use. They tutor men in treason. They feed upon the hunger of others.

Whatever defies them, they torture, especially the truth. Here, then, is joined no argument between slightly differing philosophies.

This conflict strikes directly at the faith of our fathers and the lives of our sons. No principle or treasure that we hold, from the spiritual knowledge of our free schools and churches to the creative magic of free labor and capital, nothing lies safely beyond the reach of this struggle. Freedom is pitted against slavery; lightness against the dark....

We feel this moral strength because we know that we are not helpless prisoners of history. We are free men. We shall remain free, never to be proven guilty of the one capital offense against freedom, a lack of staunch faith....

These basic precepts are not lofty abstractions, far removed from matters of daily living. They are laws of spiritual strength that generate and define our material strength.

Patriotism means equipped forces and a prepared citizenry. Moral stamina means more energy and more productivity.

Love of liberty means the guarding of every resource that makes freedom possible - from the sanctity of our families and the wealth of our soil to the genius our scientists....

This is the hope that beckons us onward in this century of trial. This is the work that awaits us all, to be done with bravery, with charity, and with prayer to Almighty God."

## 34th U.S. President
## DWIGHT DAVID EISENHOWER
JANUARY 21, 1957, SECOND INAUGURAL
ADDRESS:

"Before all else, we seek upon our common labor as a nation, the blessings of Almighty God. And the hopes in our hearts fashion the deepest prayers of our whole people....

We look upon this shaken earth, and we declare our firm and fixed purpose - the building of a peace with justice in a world where moral law prevails....

And so the prayer of our people carries far beyond our own frontiers, to the wide world of our duty and our destiny."

## 35th U.S. President
## JOHN FITZGERALD KENNEDY
JANUARY 20, 1961, INAUGURAL ADDRESS:

"For I have sworn before you and Almighty God, the same solemn oath our forbears prescribed nearly a century and three quarters ago.

The world is very different now. For man holds in his mortal hands the power to abolish all forms of human poverty and all forms of human life.

And yet the same revolutionary beliefs for which our forebears fought are still at issue around the globe - The belief that the rights of man come not from the generosity of the state but from the hand of God."

# 35th U.S. President
# JOHN FITZGERALD KENNEDY
JANUARY 20, 1961, INAUGURAL ADDRESS:

"Let every nation know, whether it wishes us well or ill, that we shall pay any price, bear any burden, meet any hardship, support any friend, oppose any foe, in order to assure the survival and the success of liberty....

Let both sides united to heed in all corners of the earth the command of Isaiah - to 'undo the heavy burdens and to let the oppressed go free.'(Is. 58:6)....

Now the trumpet summons us again - not as a call to bear arms, though arms we need; not as a call to battle, though embattled we are; but a call to bear the burden of a long twilight struggle, year in, and year out, 'rejoicing in hope, patient in tribulation'(Romans 12:12) - a struggle against the common enemies of man: tyranny, poverty, disease, and war itself....

The energy, the faith, the devotion which we bring to this endeavor will light our country and all who serve it - and the glow from that fire can truly light the world.

And so, my fellow Americans - ask not what your country can do for you - ask what you can do for your country....

Let us go forth to lead the land we love, asking His blessing and His help, but knowing that here on earth God's work must truly be our own."

## 36th U.S. President
## LYNDON BAINES JOHNSON

NOVEMBER 22, 1963, 6 P.M. EASTERN STANDARD
TIME, STATEMENT TO THE PRESS AS HE
DISEMBARKED THE AIR FORCE ONE, ANDREWS
AIR FORCE BASE OUTSIDE WASHINGTON D.C:

"This is a sad time for all people. We have suffered a loss that cannot be weighed. For me, it is a deep personal tragedy. I know that the world shares the sorrow that Mrs. Kennedy and her family bear. I will do my best. That is all I can do. I ask for your help - and God's."

## 36th U.S. President
## LYNDON BAINES JOHNSON

NOVEMBER 27, 1963, FIRST FORMAL ADDRESS
BEFORE A JOINT SESSION OF CONGRESS, WITH
MEMBERS OF THE SUPREME COURT AND OF THE
CABINET IN ATTENDANCE, DELIVERED UPON
ASSUMING THE PRESIDENCY AFTER THE DEATH
OF PRESIDENT KENNEDY:

"Let us here highly resolve that John Fitzgerald Kennedy did not live - or die - in vain. And on this Thanksgiving Eve, as we gather together to ask the Lord's blessings and give Him our thanks, let us unite in those familiar and cherished words:

America, America, God shed His grace on thee, And crown thy good, With brotherhood, From sea to shining sea."

## 36th U.S. President
## LYNDON BAINES JOHNSON

JANUARY 20, 1965, INAUGURAL ADDRESS:

"Under this covenant of justice, liberty, and union we have become a nation—prosperous, great, and mighty. And we have kept our freedom.

But we have no promise from God that our greatness will endure. We have been allowed by Him to seek greatness with the sweat of our hands and the strength of our spirit....

If we fail now, we shall have forgotten in abundance what we learned in hardship: that democracy rests on faith, that freedom asks more than it gives, and that the judgement of God is harshest on those who are most favored....

For myself, I ask only in the words of an ancient leader: 'Give me now wisdom and knowledge, that I may go out and come in before this people: for who can judge this thy people, that is so great?'

## 37th U.S. President
## RICHARD MILHOUS NIXON

JANUARY 20, 1969, FIRST INAUGURAL ADDRESS:

"Standing in this same place a third of a century ago, Franklin Delano Roosevelt addressed a nation ravaged by depression and gripped in fear. He could say in surveying the Nation's troubles: 'They concern, thank God, only material things.'...

No man can be fully free while his neighbor is not. To go forward at all is to go forward together. This means black and white together as one nation, not two.

The laws have caught up with our conscience.

What remains is to give life to what is in the law: to insure at last that as all are born equal in dignity before God, all are born equal in dignity before man."

## 37th U.S. President
## RICHARD MILHOUS NIXON

JANUARY 20, 1969, FIRST INAUGURAL ADDRESS:

"**I** have taken an oath in the presence of God and my countrymen to uphold and defend the Constitution of the United States.

To that oath I now add this sacred commitment: I shall consecrate my Office, my energies, and all the wisdom I can summon to the cause of peace among nations. Let this message be heard by strong and weak alike:

The peace we seek - the peace we seek to win - is not victory over any other people but the peace that comes 'with healing in its wings.'"

## 37th U.S. President
## RICHARD MILHOUS NIXON

JANUARY 20, 1969, FIRST INAUGURAL ADDRESS:

"**O**nly a few short weeks ago we shared the glory of man's first sight of the world as God sees it, as a single sphere reflecting light in the darkness.

As the Apollo astronauts flew over the moon's gray surface on Christmas Eve, they spoke to us of the beauty of earth - and in that voice so clear across the lunar distance, we heard them invoke God's blessing on its goodness. Let us go forward, firm in our faith, steadfast in our purpose, cautious of the dangers, but sustained by our confidence in the will of God."

## 37th U.S. President
## RICHARD MILHOUS NIXON
JANUARY, 20, 1973, SECOND INAUGURAL ADDRESS:

"**W**e have the chance today to do more than ever  before in our history to make life better in America -to ensure better education, better health, better housing, better transportation, a cleaner environment - to restore respect for law, to make our communities more livable - and to insure the God-given right of every American to full and equal opportunity....

We shall answer to God, to history, and to our conscience for the way in which we use these years."

## 37th U.S. President
## RICHARD MILHOUS NIXON
JANUARY, 20, 1973, SECOND INAUGURAL ADDRESS.:

"**T**oday, I ask your prayers that in the years ahead I may have God's help in making decisions that are right for America, and I pray for your help so that together we may be worthy of our challenge....

Let us go forward from here confident in hope, strong in our faith in one another, sustained by our faith in God who created us, and striving always to serve His purpose."

## 38th U.S. President
## GERALD RUDOLPH FORD

AUGUST 9, 1974, ON ASSUMING THE PRESIDENCY
AFTER PRESIDENT NIXON'S RESIGNATION:

"**I** am acutely aware that you have not elected me as your President by your ballots, and so I ask you to confirm me as your President with your prayers.

And I hope that such prayers will also be the first of many....

Our Constitution works; our great Republic is a Government of laws and not of men. Here the people rule. But there is a Higher Power, by whatever name we honor Him, who ordains not only righteousness but love, not only justice but mercy."

## 38th U.S. President
## GERALD RUDOLPH FORD

AUGUST 9, 1974, ADDRESS ON ASSUMING THE
PRESIDENCY:

"**A**s we bind up the internal wounds...let us restore the Golden Rule to our political process, and let brotherly love purge our hearts of suspicion and of hate. In the beginning, I asked you to pray for me.

Before closing, I ask again your prayers, for Richard Nixon and his family. May our former President, who brought peace to millions, find it for himself.

May God bless and comfort his wonderful wife and daughters, whose love and loyalty will forever be a shining legacy to all who bear the lonely burdens of the White House..."

I now solemnly reaffirm my promise I made to you last December 6; to uphold the Constitution, to do what is right as God gives me to see the right, and to do the very best I can for America.

God helping me, I will not let you down."

## 38th U.S. President
## GERALD RUDOLPH FORD

AUGUST 12, 1974, FIRST ADDRESS TO CONGRESS:

"I am not here to make an Inaugural Address. The Nation needs action, not words. Nor will this be a formal report of the State of the Union. God willing, I will have at least three more chances to do that....

I do not want a honeymoon with you. I want a good marriage."

## 39th U.S. President
## JAMES EARL "JIMMY" CARTER

JANUARY 20, 1977, INAUGURAL ADDRESS:

"Here before me is the Bible used in the inauguration of our first President in 1789, and I have just taken the oath of office on the Bible my mother gave me just a few years ago, opened to the timeless admonition from the ancient prophet Micah:

'He hath showed thee, O man, what is good; and what does the Lord require of thee, but to do justly, and to love mercy, and to walk humbly with thy God'"

## 39th U.S. President
## JAMES EARL "JIMMY" CARTER
JANUARY 20, 1977, INAUGURAL ADDRESS:

"**O**urs was the first society openly to define itself in terms of both spirituality and of human liberty.

It is that unique self-definition which has given us an exceptional appeal, but it also imposes on us a special obligation, to take on those moral duties....

I join in the hope that when my time as your President has ended, people might say this about our Nation: that we had remembered the words of Micah and renewed our search for humility, mercy, and justice."

## 40th U.S. President
## RONALD WILSON REAGAN
JANUARY 20, 1981, FIRST INAUGURAL ADDRESS:

"**Y**our dreams, your hopes, your goals are going to be the dreams, the hopes, and the goals of this administration, so help me God....

I am told that tens of thousands of prayer meetings are being held on this day, and for that I am deeply grateful. We are a nation under God, and I believe God intended for us to be free.

It would be fitting and good, I think, if on each Inauguration Day in future years it should be declared a day of prayer....

The crisis we are facing today... does require, however, our best effort, and our willingness to believe in ourselves, and to believe in our capacity to perform great deeds; to believe that together, with God's help, we can and will resolve the problems which now confront us.

And after all, why shouldn't we believe that? We are Americans. God bless you, and thank you."

## 40th U.S. President
## RONALD WILSON REAGAN

JANUARY 21, 1985, SECOND INAUGURAL ADDRESS:

"God bless you and welcome back....I wonder if we could all join in a moment of silent prayer....

This is...the 50th time that we the people have celebrated this historic occasion.

When the first President, George Washington, placed his hand upon the Bible, he stood less than a single day's journey by horseback from raw, untamed wilderness. So much has changed.

And yet we stand together as we did two centuries ago....One people under God determined that our future shall be worthy of our past."

## 41st U.S. President
## GEORGE HERBERT WALKER BUSH

JANUARY 20, 1989, INAUGURAL ADDRESS:

"I have just repeated word for word the oath taken by George Washington 200 years ago, and the Bible on which I place my hand is the Bible on which he place his....My first act as President is a prayer. I ask you to bow your heads."

## 41st U.S. President
## GEORGE HERBERT WALKER BUSH
JANUARY 20, 1989, INAUGURAL ADDRESS:

"Heavenly Father, we bow our heads and thank You for Your love. Accept our thanks for the peace that yields this day and the shared faith that makes its continuance likely. Make us strong to do Your work, willing to heed and hear Your will, and write on our hearts these words: 'Use power to help people.'

For we are given power not to advance our own purposes, nor to make a great show in the world, nor a name. There is but one just use of power, and it is to serve people. Help us to remember it, Lord. Amen."

## 41st U.S. President
## GEORGE HERBERT WALKER BUSH
JANUARY 20, 1989, INAUGURAL ADDRESS:

"There are few clear areas in which we as a society must rise up united and express our intolerance. The most obvious now is drugs. And when that first cocaine was smuggled in on a ship, it may as well have been a deadly bacteria, so much has it hurt the body, the soul of our country. And there is much to be done and to be said, but take my word for it: This scourge will stop!

And so, There is much to do; and tomorrow the work begins. I do not mistrust the future; I do not fear what is ahead. For our problems are large, but our heart is larger. Our challenges are great, but our will is greater.

And if our flaws are endless, God's love is

truly boundless. Some see leadership as high drama and the sound of trumpets calling, and sometimes it is that. But I see history as a book with many pages, and each day we fill a page with acts of hopefulness and meaning. The new breeze blows, a page turns, the story unfolds....

Thank you. God bless you and God bless the United States of America."

## 42nd U.S. President
## WILLIAM JEFFERSON "BILL" CLINTON
JANUARY 20, 1993, INAUGURAL ADDRESS:

"When our Founders boldly declared America's Independence to the world and our purposes to the Almighty, they knew that America, to endure, would have to change....

My fellow Americans, at the edge of the 21st century, let us begin with energy and hope, with faith and discipline, and let us work until our work is done.

The Scripture says, 'And let us not be weary in well-doing, for in due season, we shall reap, if we faint not.'...

With God's help, we must answer the call. Thank you and God bless you."

## 42nd U.S. President
## WILLIAM JEFFERSON "BILL" CLINTON
JANUARY 20, 1997, SECOND INAUGURAL ADDRESS:

"Our rich texture of racial, religious and political diversity will be a Godsend in the 21st Century....

Like a prophet of old, he told of his dream, that one day America would rise up and treat all its citizens as equals before the law and in the heart. Martin Luther King's dream was the American Dream....

From the height of this place and the summit of this century, let us go forth.

May God strengthen our hands for the good work ahead - and always, always bless our America."

## 43rd U.S. President
## GEORGE WALKER BUSH

JANUARY, 20, 2001, INAUGURAL ADDRESS:

"And this is my solemn pledge: I will work to build a single nation of justice and opportunity. I know this is within our reach, because we are guided by a power larger than ourselves, Who creates us equal in His image....

Compassion is the work of a nation, not just a government. And some needs and hurts are so deep they will only respond to a mentor's touch or a pastor's prayer. Church and charity, synagogue and mosque, lend our communities their humanity, and they will have an honored place in our plans and laws....

I can pledge our nation to a goal: When we see that wounded traveler on the road to Jericho, we will not pass to the other side....

Sometimes in life we are called to do great things. But as a saint of our times has said, every day we are called to do small things with great love.

The most important tasks of a democracy are done by everyone."

## 43rd U.S. President
## GEORGE WALKER BUSH

JANUARY, 20, 2001, INAUGURAL ADDRESS:

"After the Declaration of Independence was signed, Virginia statesman John Page wrote to Thomas Jefferson:

'We know the Race is not to the swift nor the Battle to the Strong. Do you not think an Angel rides in the Whirlwind and directs this Storm?'

Much time has passed since Jefferson arrived for his inaugural. The years and changes accumulate. But the themes of this day he would know: our nation's grand story of courage, and its simple dream of dignity.

We are not this story's Author, Who fills time and eternity with His purpose.

Yet His purpose is achieved in our duty; and duty is fulfilled in service to one another.

Never tiring, never yielding, never finishing, we renew that purpose today, to make our country more just and generous; to affirm the dignity of our lives and every life.

This work continues. This story goes on. This story goes on. And an angel still rides in the whirlwind and directs this storm.

God bless you, and God bless America."

# 43rd U.S. President
# GEORGE WALKER BUSH

JANUARY, 20, 2005, SECOND INAUGURAL
ADDRESS:

"After the shipwreck of communism came years of relative quite, years of repose, years of sabbatical - and then there came a day of fire.

We have seen our vulnerability - and we have seen its deepest source. For as long as whole regions of the world simmer in resentment and tyranny - prone to ideologies that feed hatred and excuse murder - violence will gather, and multiply in destructive power...

There is only one force of history that can break the reign of hatred and resentment, and expose the pretensions of tyrants, and reward the hopes of the decent and tolerant, and that is the force of human freedom...

America's vital interests and our deepest beliefs are now one. From the day of our Founding, we have proclaimed that every man and woman on this earth has rights, and dignity, and matchless value, because they bear the image of the Maker of Heaven and earth.

Across the generations we have proclaimed the imperative of self-government, because no one is fit to be a master, and no one deserves to be a slave.

Advancing these ideals is the mission that created our Nation. It is the honorable achievement of our fathers...

The rulers of outlaw regimes can know that

we still believe as Abraham Lincoln did: "Those who deny freedom to others deserve it not for themselves; and, under the rule of a just God, cannot long retain it."...

In America's ideal of freedom, the public interest depends on private character - on integrity, and tolerance toward others, and the rule of conscience in our own lives. Self-government relies, in the end, on the governing of the self.

That edifice of character is built in families, supported by communities with standards, and sustained in our national life by the truths of Sinai, the Sermon on the Mount...

We go forward with complete confidence in the eventual triumph of freedom...Not because we consider ourselves a chosen nation; God moves and chooses as He wills. We have confidence because freedom is the permanent hope of mankind, the hunger in dark places, the longing of the soul...

History has an ebb and flow of justice, but history also has a visible direction, set by liberty and the Author of Liberty.

When the Declaration of Independence was first read in public and the Liberty Bell was sounded in celebration, a witness said, "It rang as if it meant something." In our time it means something still. America, in this young century, proclaims liberty throughout all the world, and to all the inhabitants thereof.

Renewed in our strength - tested, but not weary - we are ready for the greatest achievements in the history of freedom.

May God bless you, and may He watch over the United States of America.

# ENDNOTES

**1 Massachusetts Provincial Congress,** 1774. Resolution to the inhabitants of Massachusetts Bay. Hancock, John. 1774. George Bancroft, History of the United States of America, 6 vols. (Boston: Charles C. Little and James Brown, Third Edition, 1838), Vol. II, p. 229. Lucille Johnston, Celebrations of a Nation (Arlington, VA: The Year of Thanksgiving Foundation, 1987), p. 77. Peter Marshall and David Manuel, The Light and the Glory (Old Tappan, New Jersey: Fleming H. Revell Co., 1977), p. 269.

**2 Declaration of Independence,** July 4, 1776, in Philadelphia, PA. Charles W. Eliot, LL.D., ed., American Historical Documents 1000-1904 (New York: P.F. Collier & Son Company, The Harvard Classics, 1910), Vol. 43, pp. 160-165. United States Supreme Court, Church of the Holy Trinity v. United States, 143 US 457, 458, 465-471, 36 L ed 226, (1892), Justice David Josiah Brewer. 6. "Our Christian Heritage," Letter from Plymouth Rock (Marlborough, NH: The Plymouth Rock Foundation), p. 6. D.P. Diffine, Ph.D., One Nation Under God - How Close a Separation? (Searcy, Arkansas: Harding University, Belden Center for Private Enterprise Education, 6th edition, 1992), p. 6. Stephen McDowell and Mark Beliles, "The Providential Perspective" (Charlottesville, VA: The Providence Foundation, P.O. Box 6759, Charlottesville, Va. 22906, January 1994), Vol. 9, No. 1, p. 2.

**3 Eisenhower, Dwight David.** In the magazine, Episcopal Churchnews. Edmund Fuller and David E. Green, God in the White House - The Faiths of American Presidents (NY: Crown Publishers, Inc., 1968), pp. 215-216.

**4 Declaration of Independence,** July 4, 1776, in Philadelphia, PA. Charles W. Eliot, LL.D., ed., American Historical Documents 1000-1904 (New York: P.F. Collier & Son Company, The Harvard Classics, 1910), Vol. 43, pp. 160-165. United States Supreme Court, Church of the Holy Trinity v. United States, 143 US 457, 458, 465-471, 36 L ed 226, (1892), Justice David Josiah Brewer. 6. "Our Christian Heritage," Letter from Plymouth Rock (Marlborough, NH: The Plymouth Rock Foundation), p. 6. D.P. Diffine, Ph.D., One Nation Under God - How Close a Separation? (Searcy, Arkansas: Harding University, Belden Center for Private Enterprise Education, 6th edition, 1992), p. 6. Stephen McDowell and Mark Beliles, "The Providential Perspective" (Charlottesville, VA: The Providence Foundation, P.O. Box 6759, Charlottesville, Va. 22906, January 1994), Vol. 9, No. 1, p. 2.

**5 Manion, Clarence E.** Verne Paul Kaub, Collectivism Challenges Christianity (Winona Lake, IN: Light and Life Press, 1946), p. 58. Tim

LaHaye, Faith of Our Founding Fathers (Brentwood, TN: Wolgemuth & Hyatt, Publishers, Inc., 1987), p. 65.

**6 Jefferson, Thomas.** 1781, in his Notes on the State of Virginia, Query XVIII, 1781, 1782, p. 237. Paul Leicester Ford, The Writings of Thomas Jefferson (New York: G.P. Putnam's Sons, the Knickerbocker Press, 1894), 3:267. A.A. Lipscomb and Albert Bergh, eds., The Writings of Thomas Jefferson 20 vols. (Washington, D.C.: The Thomas Jefferson Memorial Association, 1903-1904). Vol. IX, Vol. II, p. 227. Saul K. Padover, ed., The Complete Jefferson (New York: Tudor Publishing, 1943), p. 677. Robert Byrd, United States Senator from West Virginia, July 27, 1962, in a message delivered in Congress two days after the Supreme Court declared prayer in schools unconstitutional. Merrill D. Peterson, ed., Jefferson Writings (NY: Literary Classics of the United States, Inc., 1984) p. 289. Robert Flood, The Rebirth of America (Philadelphia: Arthur S. DeMoss Foundation, 1986), pp. 66-69. Tim LaHaye, Faith of Our Founding Fathers (Brentwood, TN: Wolgemuth & Hyatt, Publishers, Inc., 1987), pp. 192-193. George Grant, Third Time Around (Brentwood, TN: Wolgemuth & Hyatt, Inc., 1991), p. 103. D.P. Diffine, Ph.D., One Nation Under God - How Close a Separation? (Searcy, Arkansas: Harding University, Belden Center for Private Enterprise Education, 6th edition, 1992), p. 10. Gary DeMar, America's Christian History: The Untold Story (Atlanta, GA: American Vision Publishers, Inc., 1993), p. 56. Stephen McDowell and Mark Beliles, "The Providential Perspective" (Charlottesville, VA: The Providence Foundation, P.O. Box 6759, Charlottesville, Va. 22906, January 1994), Vol. 9, No. 1, p. 5.

**7 Hamilton, Alexander.** February 1775, in "The Farmer Refuted," Hamilton, Works, (1851). Nathan Schachner, Alexander Hamilton (NY: Barnes & Co., 1946, 1961), p. 38. p. 430. Norman Cousins, In God We Trust - The Religious Beliefs and Ideas of the American Founding Fathers (NY: Harper & Brothers, Publishers, 1955), pp. 326, 333. John Eidsmoe, Christianity and The Constitution - The Faith of Our Founding Fathers (Grand Rapids, MI: Baker Book House, 1987), p. 145.

**8 Coolidge, (John) Calvin.** October 15, 1924, at the unveiling to the Equestrian Statue of Bishop Francis Asbury, Washington, D.C. Calvin Coolidge, Foundations of the Republic - Speeches and Addresses (New York: Charles Scribner's Sons, 1926), pp. 149-155.

**9 Kennedy, John Fitzgerald.** January 20, 1961, Friday, in his Inaugural Address. Inaugural Addresses of the Presidents of the United States - From George Washington 1789 to Richard Milhous Nixon 1969 (Washington, D.C.: United States Government Printing Office; 91st Congress, 1st Session, House Document 91-142, 1969), pp. 267-270. Department of State Bulletin (published weekly by the Office of Public Services, Bureau of Public Affairs, February 6, 1961). Davis Newton Lott, The Inaugural Addresses of the American Presidents (NY: Holt, Rinehart and Winston, 1961), p. 269. Charles E. Rice, The Supreme Court and Public Prayer (New York: Fordham University Press, 1964), p. 193. Benjamin Weiss, God in American History: A Documentation of America's Religious Heritage (Grand Rapids, MI: Zondervan, 1966), p. 146. The Annals of America, 20 vols.

(Chicago, IL: Encyclopedia Britannica, 1968), Vol. XVIII, pp. 5-7. Lillian W. Kay, ed., The Ground on Which We Stand - Basic Documents of American History (NY: Franklin Watts., Inc, 1969), p. 296. Willard Cantelon, Money Master of the World (Plainfield, NJ: Logos International, 1976), p. 121-122. Bob Arnebeck, "FDR Invoked God Too," Washington Post, September 21, 1986. Vincent J. Wilson, ed., The Book of Great American Documents (Brookfield, MD: American History Research Associates, 1987), p. 84. Halford Ross Ryan, American Rhetoric from Roosevelt to Reagan (Prospect Heights, IL: Waveland Press, 1987), p. 156. Jeffrey K. Hadden and Anson Shupe, Televangelism - Power & Politics on God's Frontier (NY: Henry Holt and Company, 1988), p. 272. Ronald Reid, ed., Three Centuries of American Rhetorical Discourse: An Anthology and a Review (Prospect Heights, Il: Waveland Press, Inc., 1988), p. 711. William Safire, ed., Lend Me Your Ears - Great Speeches in History (NY: W.W. Norton & Company 1992), p. 812. Peter Marshall and David Manuel, The Glory of America (Bloomington, MN: Garborg's Heart 'N Home, Inc., 1991), 1.20. Proclaim Liberty (Dallas, TX: Word of Faith), p. 3. J. Michael Sharman, J.D., Faith of the Fathers (Culpepper, Virginia: Victory Publishing, 1995), pp. 111-112.

**10 Truman, Harry S.** February 15, 1950, at 10:05am, in an address given to the Attorney General's Conference on Law Enforcement Problems in the Department of Justice Auditorium, Washington. DC.; organizations present included the Department Of Justice, the National Association of Attorneys, the United States Conference of Lawyers, and the National Institute of Municipal Law Officers. Public Papers of the Presidents: Harry S. Truman, 1950 - Containing Public Messages, Speeches, and Statements of the President, January 1 to December 31, 1950 (Washington, DC: United States Government Printing Office, 1965) Item 37, pg. 157. Steve C. Dawson, God's Providence in America's History (Rancho Cordova, CA: Steve Dawson, 1988), p. 13:1. David Barton, The Myth of Separation (Aledo, TX: WallBuilder Press, 1991), p. 260. Gary DeMar, America's Christian History: The Untold Story (Atlanta, GA: American Vision Publishers, Inc., 1993), p. 60.

**11 Harding, Warren Gamaliel.** November 12, 1921, in an address opening the Conference in the Continental Memorial Hall in Washington, D.C. A Compilation of the Messages and Papers of the Presidents 20 vols. (New York: Bureau of National Literature, Inc., prepared under the direction of the Joint Committee on Printing, of the House and Senate, pursuant to an Act of the Fifty-Second Congress of the United States, 1893, 1923), Vol. XVIII, p. 9042.

**12 Reagan, Ronald, April 27, 1984,** comment to the Chinese community in Beijing, China. Frederick J. Ryan, Jr., ed., Ronald Reagan - The Wisdom and Honor of the Great Communicator (San Francisco: Collins Publishers, A Division of Harper Collins Publishers, 1995), p. 55.

**13 Truman, Harry S.** January 20, 1949, in his Inaugural Address. Harry S. Truman, Memoirs by Harry S. Truman - Volume Two: Years of Trial and Hope (Garden City, NY: Doubleday & Company, Inc., 1956), pp. 226-227. Inaugural Addresses of the Presidents of the United States - From George Washington 1789 to Richard

Milhous Nixon 1969 (Washington, D.C.: United States Government Printing Office; 91st Congress, 1st Session, House Document 91-142, 1969), pp. 251-256. Davis Newton Lott, The Inaugural Addresses of the American Presidents (NY: Holt, Rinehart and Winston, 1961), pp. 251-255. Charles E. Rice, The Supreme Court and Public Prayer (New York: Fordham University Press, 1964), pp. 191-192. Lillian W. Kay, ed., The Ground on Which We Stand - Basic Documents of American History (NY: Franklin Watts., Inc, 1969), p. 275. Benjamin Weiss, God in American History: A Documentation of America's Religious Heritage (Grand Rapids, MI: Zondervan, 1966), p. 141. Willard Cantelon, Money Master of the World (Plainfield, NJ: Logos International, 1976), p. 121. Proclaim Liberty (Dallas, TX: Word of Faith), p. 2. J. Michael Sharman, J.D., Faith of the Fathers (Culpepper, Virginia: Victory Publishing, 1995), pp. 102-104. T.S. Settel, and the staff of Quote, editors, The Quotable Harry Truman introduction by Merle Miller (NY: Droke House Publishers, Inc., Berkley Publishing Corporation, 1967), p. 76.
**14 Coolidge, (John) Calvin.** September 21, 1924, in an address to the Holy Name Society, Washington, D.C. Calvin Coolidge, Foundations of the Republic - Speeches and Addresses (New York: Charles Scribner's Sons, 1926), pp. 103-112.
**15 Roosevelt, Franklin D.,** March 16, 1940, Radio Address for the Christian Foreign Service Convocation. The Faith of FDR - From President Franklin D. Roosevelt's Public Papers 1933-1945.
**16 Taft, William Howard.** 1908, in a speech at a missionary conference. Edmund Fuller and David E. Green, God in the White House - The Faiths of American Presidents (NY: Crown Publishers, Inc., 1968), p. 173
**17 Webster, Daniel.** June 17, 1843, in his Speech at Bunker Hill Monument, Charlestown, Massachusetts. Burton Stevenson, The Home Book of Quotations - Classical & Modern (New York: Dodd, Mead and Company, 1967), p. 158. Peter Marshall and David Manuel, The Glory of America (Bloomington, MN: Garborg's Heart'N Home, Inc., 1991), 8.8. Stephen Abbott Northrop, D.D., A Cloud of Witnesses (Portland, OR: American Heritage Ministries, 1987; Mantle Ministries, 228 Still Ridge, Bulverde, Texas), p. 491. D.P. Diffine, Ph.D., One Nation Under God - How Close a Separation? (Searcy, Arkansas: Harding University, Belden Center for Private Enterprise Education, 6th edition, 1992), p. 12.
**18 Harrison, William Henry.** March 4, 1841, Thursday, in his Inaugural Address. James D. Richardson (U.S. Representative from Tennessee), ed., A Compilation of the Messages and Papers of the Presidents 1789-1897, 10 vols. (Washington, D.C.: U.S. Government Printing Office, published by Authority of Congress, 1897, 1899; Washington, D.C.: Bureau of National Literature and Art, 1789-1902, 11 vols., 1907, 1910), Vol. 4, pp. 6-20. Benjamin Franklin Morris, The Christian Life and Character of the Civil Institutions of the United States (Philadelphia: George W. Childs, 1864), p. 605. Inaugural Addresses of the Presidents of the United States - From George Washington 1789 to Richard Milhous Nixon 1969 (Washington, D.C.: United States Government Printing Office; 91st Congress, 1st Session, House Document 91-142, 1969), pp. 71-87. Davis Newton Lott, The Inaugural Addresses

of the American Presidents (NY: Holt, Rinehart and Winston, 1961), p. 86. Charles E. Rice, The Supreme Court and Public Prayer (New York: Fordham University Press, 1964), p. 182. Arthur Schlesinger Jr., ed., The Chief Executive (NY: Chelsea House Publishers, 1965), pp. 93-94. Stephen Abbott Northrop, D.D., A Cloud of Witnesses (Portland, Oregon: American Heritage Ministries, 1987; Mantle Ministries, 228 Still Ridge, Bulverde, Texas), p. 215. Peter Marshall and David Manuel, The Glory of America (Bloomington, MN: Garborg's Heart 'N Home, Inc., 1991), 4.4. J. Michael Sharman, J.D., Faith of the Fathers (Culpepper, Virginia: Victory Publishing, 1995), pp. 43-44.

**19 Hoover, Herbert Clark.** September 17, 1935, in a speech in San Diego, California. Charles Hurd, ed., A Treasury of Great American Speeches (NY: Hawthorne Books, 1959), pp. 229-231.

**20 Reagan, Ronald Wilson.** 1983, in The Human Life Review. Ronald Reagan, "Abortion and the Conscience of a Nation," (Nashville, TN: Thomas Nelson, Inc., 1984), pp. 15-38.

**21 Darwin, Charles. Descent of Man, (1871)**, Chapter VI - On the Affinities and Genealogy of Man, http://www.literature.org/authors/darwin-charles/the-descent-of-man/chapter-06.html

**22 United States Supreme Court,** DRED SCOTT v. JOHN F. A. SANDFORD (March 1857), Chief Justice Roger B. Taney, http://odur.let.rug.nl/~usa/D/1851-1875/dredscott/dred3.htm

**23 Sanger, Margaret. Pivot of Civilization, (1922)**, http://www.textlibrary.com/download/pivot.txt http://onlinebooks.library.upenn.edu/webbin/gutbook/lookup?num=1689 Washington Summit Publishers P. O. Box 3415 Augusta, GA 30914

**24 Hitler, Adolph.** Mein Kampf. Nazi, Office for Race and Colonization (RuSHA), http://cghs.dade.k12.fl.us/holocaust/jewish_question.htm http://www.bofhlet.net/tasteless/13/kampf.htm

**25 Stalin, Joseph.** http://www.infoukes.com/history/ww2/page-04.html http://www.artukraine.com/famineart/vitvitsky.htm

**26 Zedong, Mao.** http://users.erols.com/mwhite28/warstat1.htm Source List and Detail Death Tolls for the Twentieth Century Hemoclysm

**27 Jihad.** FrontpageMagazine.com, February 21, 2007, The Infidel Revolution, Jamie Glazov, interview with Bill Warner, http://frontpagemag.com/articles/read.aspx?GUID+BD353E11-0000-4BBB-9617-603119B0BFE6 November 8, 2007, CSPI-Center for the Study of Political Islam, www.socialdailynews.com/2007/11/islam-270-million-bodies-in-1400-years/ www.jihadwatch.org/dhimmiwatch/archives/003471.php www.politicalislam.com/blog/tears-of-jihad/ Killed in jihad since AD 622: 120 Africans, 80 million Hindus, 60 million Christians, 10 million Buddhists, 1 million est. Jews. Thomas Sowell, Race and Culture (BasicBooks, 1994), p. 188; David Livingstone (Woman's Presbyterian Board of Missions, 1888), p. 62; David B Barrett & Todd M. Johnson, World Christian Trends AD 30-2200 (William Carey Library 2001), p. 230, tables 4-1, 4-10; Raphael Moore,

History of Asia Minor; Koenard Elst, Negationism in India (New Delhi: Voice of India, 2002), p. 34;

**28 Truman, Harry S.** January 20, 1949, in his Inaugural Address. Harry S. Truman, Memoirs by Harry S. Truman - Volume Two: Years of Trial and Hope (Garden City, NY: Doubleday & Company, Inc., 1956), pp. 226-227. Inaugural Addresses of the Presidents of the United States - From George Washington 1789 to Richard Milhous Nixon 1969 (Washington, D.C.: United States Government Printing Office; 91st Congress, 1st Session, House Document 91-142, 1969), pp. 251-256. Davis Newton Lott, The Inaugural Addresses of the American Presidents (NY: Holt, Rinehart and Winston, 1961), pp. 251-255. Charles E. Rice, The Supreme Court and Public Prayer (New York: Fordham University Press, 1964), pp. 191-192. Lillian W. Kay, ed., The Ground on Which We Stand - Basic Documents of American History (NY: Franklin Watts., Inc, 1969), p. 275. Benjamin Weiss, God in American History: A Documentation of America's Religious Heritage (Grand Rapids, MI: Zondervan, 1966), p. 141. Willard Cantelon, Money Master of the World (Plainfield, NJ: Logos International, 1976), p. 121. Michael Sharman, J.D., Faith of the Fathers (Culpepper, Virginia: Victory Publishing, 1995), pp. 102-104. T.S. Settel, and the staff of Quote, editors, The Quotable Harry Truman introduction by Merle Miller (NY: Droke House Publishers, Inc., Berkley Publishing Corporation, 1967), p. 76..

**29 Coolidge, (John) Calvin.** July 5, 1926, at a celebration of the 150th anniversary of the Declaration of Independence, Philadelphia. Calvin Coolidge, Foundations of the Republic - Speeches and Addresses (New York: Charles Scribner's Sons, 1926), pp. 441-454. Charles Wallis, ed., Our American Heritage (NY: Harper & Row, Publishers, Inc., 1970), p. 29.

**30 Adams, John.** October 11, 1798, in a letter to the officers of the First Brigade of the Third Division of the Militia of Massachusetts. Charles Francis Adams (son of John Quincy Adams and grandson of John Adams), ed., The Works of John Adams - Second President of the United States: with a Life of the Author, Notes, and Illustration (Boston: Little, Brown, & Co., 1854), Vol. IX, pp. 228-229. Charles E. Rice, The Supreme Court and Public Prayer (New York: Fordham University Press, 1964), p. 47. Senator A. Willis Robertson, "Report on Prayers in Public Schools and Other Matters, Senate Committee on the Judiciary (87th Congress, 2nd Session), 1962, 32. Richard John Neuhaus, The Naked Public Square (Grand Rapids, MI: William B. Eerdman Publishing Company, 1984), p. 95. War on Religious Freedom (Virginia Beach, Virginia: Freedom Council, 1984), p. 1. A. James Reichley, Religion in American Public Life (Washington, D.C.: The Brookings Institute, 1985), p. 105. Pat Robertson, America's Dates With Destiny (Nashville, TN: 1986), pp. 93-95. Charles Colson, Kingdoms in Conflict (Grand Rapids, MI: Zondervan Publishing House, 1987), pp. 47, 120. Tim LaHaye, Faith of Our Founding Fathers (Brentwood, TN: Wolgemuth & Hyatt, Publishers, Inc., 1987), p. 194. John Eidsmoe, Christianity and the Constitution - The Faith of Our Founding Fathers (Grand Rapids, MI: Baker Book House, A Mott Media Book, 1987; 6th printing, 1993), pp. 273, 292, 381. Gary DeMar, "Is the Constitution

Christian?" (Atlanta, GA: The Biblical Worldview, An American Vision Publication - American Vision, Inc., December 1989), p. 2. Peter Marshall and David Manuel, The Glory of America (Bloomington, MN: Garborg's Heart 'N Home, 1991), 8.11. Kerby Anderson, "Christian Roots of the Declaration" (Dallas, TX: Freedom Club Report, July 1993), p. 6. Rush H. Limbaugh III, See, I Told You So (New York, NY: reprinted by permission of Pocket Books, a division of Simon & Schuster Inc., 1993), pp. 73-76. Stephen McDowell and Mark Beliles, "The Providential Perspective" (Charlottesville, VA: The Providence Foundation, P.O. Box 6759, Charlottesville, Va. 22906, January 1994), Vol. 9, No. 1, p. 4.

**31 Adams, John Quincy.** September 1811, in a letter to his son written while serving as U.S. Minister in St. Petersburg, Russia. James L. Alden, Letters of John Quincy Adams to His Son on the Bible and Its Teachings (1850), pp. 6-21. Henry H. Halley, Halley's Bible Handbook (Grand Rapids, MI: Zondervan Publishing House, 1927, 1965), p. 19. Verna M. Hall, The Christian History of the American Revolution - Consider and Ponder (San Francisco: Foundation for American Christian Education, 1976), pp. 615-616. Verna M. Hall and Rosalie J. Slater, The Bible and the Constitution of the United States of America (San Francisco: Foundation for American Christian Education, 1983), p. 17. Tim LaHaye, Faith of Our Founding Fathers (Brentwood, TN: Wolgemuth & Hyatt, Publishers, Inc., 1987), pp. 90-91. D.P. Diffine, Ph.D., One Nation Under God - How Close a Separation? (Searcy, Arkansas: Harding University, Belden Center for Private Enterprise Education, 6th edition, 1992), p. 6.

**32 McGuffey, William Holmes.** William Ellery Channing, "Religion The Only Basis of Society" William Holmes McGuffey, McGuffey's Fifth Eclectic Reader (Cincinnati and New York: Van Antwerp, Bragg & Co., revised edition, 1879), lesson XCIII, pp. 284-286.

**33 McHenry, James.** Bernard Steiner, One Hundred and Ten Years of Bible Society in Maryland (Maryland: Maryland Bible Society, 1921), p. 14. Tim LaHaye, Faith of Our Founding Fathers (Brentwood, TN: Wolgemuth & Hyatt, Publishers, Inc., 1987), pp. 171-172. Peter Marshall & David Manuel, The Glory of America (Bloomington, MN: Garborg's Heart 'N Home, 1991), 8.17.

**34 Wayland, Francis.** Tryon Edwards, D.D., The New Dictionary of Thoughts - A Cyclopedia of Quotations (Garden City, NY: Hanover House, 1852; revised and enlarged by C.H. Catrevas, Ralph Emerson Browns and Jonathan Edwards [descendent, along with Tryon, of Jonathan Edwards (1703-1758), president of Princeton], 1891; The Standard Book Company, 1955, 1963), p. 47.

**35 Winthrop, Robert Charles.** May 28, 1849, in an address, entitled "Either by the Bible or the Bayonet," at the Annual Meeting of the Massachusetts Bible Society in Boston. Addresses and Speeches on Various Occasions (Boston: Little, Brown & Company, 1852), p. 172. Benjamin Franklin Morris, The Christian Life and Character of the Civil Institutions of the United States (Philadelphia, PA: L. Johnson & Co., 1863; George W. Childs, 1864), pp. 227-228. Stephen McDowell and Mark Beliles, "The Providential Perspective" (Charlottesville, VA:

The Providence Foundation, P.O. Box 6759, Charlottesville, Va. 22906, January 1994), Vol. 9, No. 1, p. 1. Verna M. Hall, The Christian History of the American Revolution (San Francisco: Foundation for American Christian Education, 1976), p. 20. Marshall Foster and Mary-Elaine Swanson, The American Covenant - The Untold Story (Roseburg, OR: Foundation for Christian Self-Government, 1981; Thousand Oaks, CA: The Mayflower Institute, 1983, 1992), p. 7. Gary DeMar, America's Christian History: The Untold Story (Atlanta, GA: American Vision Publishers, Inc., 1993), p. 58. John Whitehead, The Separation Illusion (Milford, Michigan: Mott Media, 1977), p. 90.

**36 Burke, Edmund.** 1791, in "A Letter to a Member of the National Assembly." Theodore Roosevelt, "Fifth Annual Message to Congress," December 5, 1905. A Compilation of the Messages and Papers of the Presidents 20 vols. (New York: Bureau of National Literature, Inc., prepared under the direction of the Joint Committee on Printing, of the House and Senate, pursuant to an Act of the Fifty-Second Congress of the United States, 1893, 1923), Vol. XIV, p. 6986. Keith Fournier, In Defense of Liberty (Virginia Beach, VA: Law & Justice, 1993), Vol. 2, No. 2, p. 5. Rush H. Limbaugh III, See, I Told You So (New York, NY: reprinted by permission of Pocket Books, a division of Simon & Schuster Inc., 1993), pp. 73-76.

**37 Adams, Samuel.** February 12, 1779, letter to James Warren. Harry Alonzo Cushing, editor, The Writings of Samuel Adams (New York: G.P. Putnam's Sons, 1905), Vol. IV, p. 124. Rosalie J. Slater, Teaching and Learning America's Christian Heritage (San Francisco: Foundation for American Christian Education, American Revolution Bicentennial edition, 1975), p. 251. Verna M. Hall, The Christian History of the Constitution of the United States of America - Christian Self-Government with Union (San Francisco: Foundation for American Christian Education, 1976), p. 4. Stephen K. McDowell and Mark A. Beliles, America's Providential History (Charlottesville, VA: Providence Press, 1988), pp. 148, 179. Peter Marshall and David Manuel, The Glory of America (Bloomington, MN: Garborg's Heart'N Home, Inc., 1991), 9.27.

**38 Taft, William Howard.** 1908, in a speech at a missionary conference. Edmund Fuller and David E. Green, God in the White House - The Faiths of American Presidents (NY: Crown Publishers, Inc., 1968), p. 173.

**39 Webster, Daniel.** Tim LaHaye, Faith of Our Founding Fathers (Brentwood, TN: Wolgemuth & Hyatt, Publishers, Inc., 1987), p. 199. "The most important thought I ever had was that of my individual responsibility to God." Bless Your Heart (series II) (Eden Prairie, MN: Heartland Sampler, Inc., 1990), 8.28.

**40 Franklin, Benjamin.** March 9, 1790, in a letter to Ezra Stiles, President of Yale University. Jared Sparks, editor, The Works of Benjamin Franklin (Boston: Tappan, Whittmore and Mason, 1838), Vol. X, p. 424. Tryon Edwards, D.D., The New Dictionary of Thoughts - A Cyclopedia of Quotations (Garden City, NY: Hanover House, 1852; revised and enlarged by C.H. Catrevas, Ralph Emerson Browns and Jonathan Edwards [descendent, along with Tryon, of Jonathan Edwards (1703-1758), president of Princeton], 1891; The Standard Book Company, 1955, 1963),

p. 91. Albert Henry Smyth, ed., The Writings of Benjamin Franklin (New York: MacMillan, 1905-7), Vol. 10, p. 84. John Bigelow, Complete Words of Benjamin Franklin. Stephen Abbott Northrop, D.D., A Cloud of Witnesses (Portland, OR: American Heritage Ministries, 1987; Mantle Ministries, 228 Still Ridge, Bulverde, Texas), p. 159. Carl Van Dorn, ed., The Autobiography of Benjamin Franklin (NY: Viking Press, 1945), p. 783. Norman Cousins, In God We Trust - The Religious Beliefs and Ideas of the American Founding Fathers (NY: Harper & Brothers, Publishers, 1955), p. 42. Frank B. Carlson, Our Presbyterian Heritage, (1973), p. 25. Raymond A. St. John, American Literature for Christian Schools (Greenville, SC: Bob Jones University Press, Inc., 1979), p. 131. Tim LaHaye, Faith of Our Founding Fathers (Brentwood, TN: Wolgemuth & Hyatt, Publishers, Inc., 1987), p. 116. John Eidsmoe, Christianity and The Constitution - The Faith of Our Founding Fathers (Grand Rapids, MI: Baker Book House, 1987), p. 210. D.P. Diffine, Ph.D., One Nation Under God - How Close a Separation? (Searcy, Arkansas: Harding University, Belden Center for Private Enterprise Education, 6th edition, 1992), p. 8. Henry M. Morris, "Sweet Land of Liberty" (El Cajon, CA: Institute for Creation Research, Back to Genesis, No. 91, July 1996), p. a.

**41 Franklin, Benjamin.** Leonard Labaree, ed., The Papers of Benjamin Franklin (New Haven: Yale University Press, 1959), Vol. I, p. 213. Tim LaHaye, Faith of Our Founding Fathers (Brentwood, TN: Wolgemuth & Hyatt, Publishers, Inc., 1987), p. 120.

**42 Adams, John.** January 13, 1815, in a letter to Judge F.A. Van der Kemp. Norman Cousins, In God We Trust - The Religious Beliefs and Ideas of the American Founding Fathers (NY: Harper & Brothers, 1958), p. 104.

**43 Adams, John.** December 27, 1816, in a letter to Judge F.A. Van de Kemp. Norman Cousins, In God We Trust - The Religious Beliefs and Ideas of the American Founding Fathers (NY: Harper & Brothers, 1958), pp. 104-105. John Eidsmoe, Christianity and the Constitution - The Faith of Our Founding Fathers (Grand Rapids, MI: Baker Book House, A Mott Media Book, 1987; 6th printing, 1993), p. 286. Gary DeMar, "Why the Religious Right is Always Right - Almost" (Atlanta, GA: The Biblical Worldview, An American Vision Publication - American Vision, Inc., November 1992), p. 6. Gary DeMar, America's Christian History: The Untold Story (Atlanta, GA: American Vision Publishers, Inc., 1993), p. 95.

**44 Adams, John.** March 6, 1799, in a Proclamation of a National Day of Humiliation, Fasting, and Prayer. James D. Richardson (U.S. Representative from Tennessee), ed., A Compilation of the Messages and Papers of the Presidents 1789-1897, 10 vols. (Washington, D.C.: U.S. Government Printing Office, published by Authority of Congress, 1897, 1899; Washington, D.C.: Bureau of National Literature and Art, 1789-1902, 11 vols., 1907, 1910), Vol. 1, pp. 284-286. Benjamin Franklin Morris, The Christian Life and Character of the Civil Institutions of the United States (Philadelphia: George W. Childs, 1864), pp. 547-548. Gary DeMar, The Biblical Worldview (Atlanta, GA: An American Vision Publication - American Vision, Inc., 1992), Vol. 8, No. 12, p. 9. Gary DeMar, America's Christian History: The

Endnotes

Untold Story (Atlanta, GA: American Vision Publishers, Inc., 1993), p. 78. Stephen McDowell and Mark Beliles, "The Providential Perspective" (Charlottesville, VA: The Providence Foundation, P.O. Box 6759, Charlottesville, Va. 22906, January 1994), Vol. 9, No. 1, pp. 4, 6.

**45 Lincoln, Abraham**, November 25, 1862, to Rev. Byron Sunderland, pastor of the First Presbyterian Church, Washington, DC:., as recorded in a letter to Rev. J.A. Reed. Scribner's Monthly (July 1873), p. 342. William J. Johnson, Abraham Lincoln, The Christian (NY: The Abington Press, 1913), pp. 101-102. Peter Marshall and David Manuel, The Glory of America (Bloomington, MN: Garborg's Heart'N Home, Inc., 1991), 11.14, 12.26.

**46 Pennsylvania, Constitution of.** 1776, Frame of Government, Chapter 2, Section 10. The Constitutions of the Several Independent States of America (Boston: Norman and Bowen, 1785), p. 81. S.E. Morison, ed., Sources and Documents Illustrating the American Revolution 1764-1788 and the Formation of the Federal Constitution (NY: Oxford University Press, 1923), p. 166. Benjamin Franklin Morris, The Christian Life and Character of the Civil Institutions of the United States (Philadelphia, PA: L. Johnson & Co., 1863; George W. Childs, 1864), p. 233.

**47 South Carolina, Constitution of.** 1778, Article XII, The Constitutions of the Several Independent States of America (Boston: Norman and Bowen, 1785), South Carolina, 1776, Section 13, p. 146. Frances Newton Thorpe, ed., Federal and State Constitutions, Colonial Charters, and Other Organic Laws of the States, Territories, and Colonies now or heretofore forming the United States, 7 vols. (Washington: Government Printing Office, 1905; 1909; St. Clair Shores, MI: Scholarly Press, 1968). Edwin S. Gaustad, Neither King nor Prelate - Religion and the New Nation, 1776-1826 (Grand Rapids, MI: William B. Eerdmans Publishing Company, 1993), p. 171.

**48 South Carolina, Constitution of.** 1790, Article XXXVIII. The Constitutions of the Several Independent States of America, Published by Order of Congress (Boston: Norman & Bowen, 1785) p. 152.

**49 Mississippi, Constitution of.** 1817. Supreme Court Justice David Josiah Brewer, who served 1890-1910, in his work, The United States - Christian Nation (Philadelphia: The John C. Winston Company, 1905, Supreme Court Collection).

**50 Pennsylvania Supreme Court.** 1817. The Commonwealth v. Wolf, 3 Serg.& R. 48, 50 (1817).

**51 Maryland, Constitution of.** 1851, Supreme Court Justice David Josiah Brewer, who served 1890-1910, in his work, The United States - A Christian Nation (Philadelphia: The John C. Winston Company, 1905, Supreme Court Collection). "Our Christian Heritage," Letter from Plymouth Rock (Marlborough, NH: The Plymouth Rock Foundation), p. 6.

**52 Constitution of Maryland.** 1864, Benjamin Franklin Morris, The Christian Life and Character of the Civil Institutions of the United States (Philadelphia: George W. Childs, 1864). Supreme Court Justice David Josiah Brewer, who served 1890-1910, in his work, The United States - Christian Nation (Philadelphia: The

John C. Winston Company, 1905, Supreme Court Collection). "Our Christian Heritage," Letter from Plymouth Rock (Marlborough, NH: The Plymouth Rock Foundation), p. 6.

**53 Tennessee, Constitution of.** 1870, Article IX, Section 2. Charles E. Rice, The Supreme Court and Public Prayer (New York: Fordham University Press, 1964), p. 175; "Hearings, Prayers in Public Schools and Other Matters," Committee on the Judiciary, U.S. Senate (87th Cong., 2nd Sess.), 1962, pp. 268 et seq.

**54 Blackstone, Sir William.** Commentaries on the Laws of England,1765-1770. Wendell's Blackstone's Commentaries, Vol. IV, p. 43. Stephen Abbott Northrop, D.D., A Cloud of Witnesses (Portland, Oregon: American Heritage Ministries, 1987; Mantle Ministries, 228 Still Ridge, Bulverde, Texas), p. 33.

**55 Reagan, Ronald Wilson.** August 23, 1984 at an ecumenical prayer breakfast at the Reunion Arena in Dallas, on the occasion of the enactment of the Equal Access Bill of 1984. Jeremiah O'Leary, "Reagan Declares that Faith Has Key Role in Political Life," The Washington Times (August 24, 1984). Walter Shapiro, "Politics and the Pulpit," Newsweek (September 17, 1984), p. 24. The Speech That Shook The Nation (Forerunner, December 1984), p. 12. Nadine Strossen, "A Constitutional Analysis of the Equal Access Act's Standards Governing School Student's Religious Meetings," Harvard Journal on Legislation, Winter, 1987. p. 118. David R. Shepherd, Ronald Reagan: In God We Trust (Wheaton, IL: Tyndale House Publishers, Inc., 1984), p. 146.

**56 Linn, William.** May 1, 1789, as U.S. House Chaplain. Dickinson W. Adams, ed., Jefferson's Extracts from the Gospels (Princeton: Princeton University Press, 1983), p. 11. Quoting from William Linn, Serious Considerations on the Election of a President: Addressed to the Citizens of the United States (NY: 1800), p. 19. "Our Christian Heritage," Letter from Plymouth Rock (Marlborough, NH: The Plymouth Rock Foundation), p. 4.

**57 McGuffey, William Holmes.** William Ellery Channing, "Religion The Only Basis of Society" William Holmes McGuffey, McGuffey's Fifth Eclectic Reader (Cincinnati and New York: Van Antwerp, Bragg & Co., revised edition, 1879), lesson XCIII, pp. 284-286.

**58 Henry, Patrick.** Tryon Edwards, D.D., The New Dictionary of Thoughts - A Cyclopedia of Quotations (Garden City, NY: Hanover House, 1852; revised and enlarged by C.H. Catrevas, Ralph Emerson Browns and Jonathan Edwards [descendent, along with Tryon, of Jonathan Edwards (1703-1758), president of Princeton], 1891; The Standard Book Company, 1955, 1963), p. 337.

**59 Adams, John.** April 19, 1817, in a letter to Thomas Jefferson. Norman Cousins, In God We Trust - The Religious Beliefs and Ideas of the American Founding Fathers (NY: Harper & Brothers, 1958), p. 282. Edmund Fuller and David E. Green, God in the White House - The Faiths of American Presidents (NY: Crown Publishers, Inc., 1968), p. 26. Richard K. Arnold, ed., Adams to Jefferson/Jefferson to Adams - A Dialogue from their Correspondence (San Francisco: Jerico Press, 1975), p. 25.

**60 Bradley, Omar.** November 11, 1948, in an address he delivered on Armistice

Day, or Veteran's Day. John Bartlett, Bartlett's Familiar Quotations (Boston: Little, Brown and Company, 1855, 1980), p. 825.

**61 Wilson, James**, U.S. Supreme Court Justice, appointed by George Washington, in his lectures at the College of Philadelphia on the "Will of God." James DeWitt andres, Words of Wilson (Chicago, 1896), 1:91-93. Charles Page Smith, James Wilson Founding Father (Chapel Hill University of North Carolina Press, 1956), p. 331. John Eidsmoe, Christianity and the Constitution - The Faith of Our Founding Fathers (Grand Rapids, MI: Baker Book House, A Mott Media Book, 1987, 6th printing, 1993), pp. 45.

**62 Washington, George.** 1745. 110 Rules of Civility and Decent Behavior in Company and Conversation - copied in his own handwriting. Moncure D. Conway, George Washington's Rules of Civility (1890), pp. 178, 180. (also Bedford, MA: Apple Books, 1988, distributed by the Globe Pequot Press, Chester, CT, p. 30). William J. Johnson, George Washington - The Christian (St. Paul, MN: William J. Johnson, Merriam Park, February 23, 1919, Nashville, TN, Abington Press, 1919, reprinted Milford, MI: Mott Media, 1976, reprinted Arlington Heights, IL: Christian Liberty Press, 502 West Euclid Ave., Arlington, IL 60004, 1992), p. 20.

**63 "Skeptical Supreme Court weighs Pledge case** - Justices debate whether saying 'under God' is reciting a prayer," From Bill Mears, CNN Washington Bureau, Wednesday, March 24, 2004 Posted: 9:15 PM EST (0215 GMT), http://www.cnn.com/2004/LAW/03/24/scotus.pledge/

**64 "Commandments removed amid protests** - Dozens delay judge's order Tuesday," June 10, 2003, By Marie McCain and Dan Horn, The Cincinnati Enquirer http://www.enquirer.com/editions/2003/06/10/loc_commandments10.html

**65 "The Constitutional Principle: Separation of Church and State**, School prayer decisions," Research and writing by Susan Batte http://members.tripod.com/~candst/pray2a.htm "School Prayer And Religious Liberty: A Constitutional Perspective" 9/1/2000, by Laurel MacLeod http://www.cwfa.org/articledisplay.asp?id=1266&department=CWA&categoryid=freedom

**66 The Rutherford Institute** Urges President Bush to Take a Stand for American Veterans, Patrick Cubbage & 'God Bless America' 09/17/2003, Contact Info: Nisha N. Mohammed Ph: (434) 978-3888, ext. 604; Pager: 800-946-4646, Pin #: 1478257 Email: Nisha N. Mohammed, http://www.rutherford.org/articles_db/press_release.asp?article_id=447

**67 "Federal judge sides with librarian fired for wearing cross necklace,"** By The Associated Press, 9/4/03, http://www.firstamendmentcenter.org/news.aspx?id=11889 "Library Worker Claims She Was Fired for Wearing a Cross" Former Logan County (Ky.) Library worker Kimberly Draper filed suit February 1 in U.S. District Court in Bowling Green, Kentucky, charging that Director Linda Kompanik fired her in April 2001 for continuing to wear a cross necklace on the job despite orders not to do so. Draper is represented by the American Center for Law and Justice, a conservative nonprofit law group founded by Pat Robertson. Kompanik and Assistant Director Sheryl Appling are named as defendants, along with the library itself. The suit contends that 45 days after she was hired in August 1998, Draper learned of a written dress code policy forbidding "religious, political, or potentially offensive decoration," although she was assured on being hired that she could wear a cross necklace to work. Because she twice refused Appling's order in April 2001 to remove the necklace, Kompanik fired her April 16, the suit alleges. Plaintiff attorney Francis Manion characterized as "troubling" a policy "that equates a religious symbol with being offensive." Although the library tries to honor diversity by keeping staffers from professing "a different religious point of view" than a patron, Kompanik countered, "it was something else" that led to Draper's dismissal. "Unfortunately, [Draper] can say whatever she wants," Kompanik told the Associated Press February 4, declining to elaborate. http:// archive.ala.org/alonline/news/2002/020211.html.

**68 Reproductive Rights**. Since its inception in 1920, the ACLU has recognized that personal privacy and reproductive rights are among our most important constitutional liberties. ACLU Challenges First-Ever Federal Abortion Ban, ACLU Challenges First-Ever Federal Abortion BanACLU Commends the Courage and Commitment of Abortion Providers On National Day of Appreciation http://www. aclu.org/ReproductiveRights/ReproductiveRightsmain.cfm http://www.aclu.org/ marchforwomenhttp://www.aclu.org/marchforwomen SAVE WOMEN'S LIVES: MARCH FOR FREEDOM OF CHOICE

**69 "ACLU president to speak on pornography** and the Internet," CONTACT: Elaine C. Ray, News Service (650) 723-7162; e-mail elaineray@stanford.edu http://www.stanford.edu/dept/news/pr/98/980309strossen.html "WHY THE ACLU OPPOSES CENSORSHIP OF 'PORNOGRAPHY'" http://www.eff.org/ Censorship/aclu_opposes_porno_censorship.article

**70 "ACLU of Utah to Join Polygamists** in Bigamy Fight," July 16, 1999. http:// archive.aclu.org/news/1999/w071699b.html

**71 ACLU to Defend NAMBLA** Associated Press, Aug. 31, 2000 BOSTON — The American Civil Liberties Union will represent a group that advocates sex between men and boys in a lawsuit brought by the family of a slain 10-year-old. The family of Jeffrey Curley of Cambridge said the North American Man/Boy Love Association and its web site which is now off-line incited the attempted molestation and murder of the boy on Oct. 1, 1997. One of two men convicted in the killing, Charles Jaynes, 25, reportedly viewed the group's web site shortly before the killing, and also had in his possession some of NAMBLA's publications. Also convicted in the killing was 24-year-old Salvatore Sicari. The ACLU said the case, filed in federal court in mid-May, involves issues of freedom of speech and association. "For us, it is a fundamental First Amendment case," John Roberts, executive director of the Massachusetts branch of the ACLU, told Boston Globe Wednesday. "It has to do with communications on a web site, and material that does not promote any kind of criminal behavior whatsoever." ACLU officials said NAMBLA members deny encouraging coercion, rape or violence. Attorney Lawrence Frisoli, who represents the Curleys, said he is glad the ACLU is defending

NAMBLA, because he has had trouble locating the group's members. Harvey Silverglate, an ACLU board member, said Wednesday that the group's attorneys will try to block any attempt by the Curleys to get NAMBLA's membership lists, or other materials identifying members. The ACLU also will act as a surrogate for NAMBLA, allowing its members to defend themselves in court while remaining anonymous. According to the Globe, NAMBLA officials in the past have said their main goal is the abolition of age-of-consent laws that classify sex with children as rape. At two separate trials last year, prosecutors said Jaynes and Sicari were sexually obsessed with the boy, lured him from his Cambridge neighborhood with the promise of a new bike, and then smothered him with a gasoline-soaked rag when he resisted their sexual advances. They then stuffed him into a concrete-filled container and dumped it into a Maine river. Sicari, convicted of first-degree murder, is serving a life sentence without the possibility of parole. Jaynes' second-degree murder and kidnapping convictions enable him to seek parole in 23 years. The Curleys last week were awarded $328 million by a superior court jury in a civil suit against Jaynes and Sicari. Copyright (c) 2000 The Associated Press http:// www.operationlookout.org/lookoutmag/aclu_to_defend_nambla.htm ACLU to Defend Pedophile Group Associated Press Aug.31.2000 http://www.nostatusquo. com/ACLU/Rage/NAMBLARAGEPAGE.html

**72 "Religion." The Random House Dictionary of the English Language** - The Unabridged Edition (New York: Random House, Inc., 1966, 1973), p. 1212.

**73 "Religion." Webster's New World Dictionary** of the English Language - Deluxe Concise Edition, David B. Guralnik, General Editor (NY: Rand McNally & Company, 1966), p. 627.

**74 "Belief." The Random House Dictionary** of the English Language - The Unabridged Edition (New York: Random House, Inc., 1966, 1973), p. 135.

**75 United States Supreme Court.** 1963, in the case of School District of Abington Township v. Schempp, 374 U.S. 203, 212, 225, 83 S. Ct. 1560, 10 L. Ed. 2d 844 (1963), pp. 21, 71. Bill Gothard, Applying Basic Principles-Supplementary Alumni Book (Oak Brook, IL: Institute of Basic Youth Conflicts, 1984), p. 3. Associate Justice Tom Clark writing the Court's opinion, Justice William Joseph Brennan, Jr. concurring. Jay Sekulow, Letter to School Superintendents (Virginia Beach, VA: American Center for Law and Justice, November 17, 1992), p. 1. Religion in the Public School Curriculum - Questions and Answers (available from the Christian Legal Society, P.O. Box 1492, Merrifield, Va. 22116.), pp. 1-2. John Whitehead, The Rights of Religious Persons in Public Education, p. 191. Elizabeth Ridenour, Public Schools - Bible Curriculum (Greensboro, N.C.: National Council On Bible Curriculum, 1996), p. 13, 21, 23, 28, 39, 41.

**76 United States District Court.** 1983, Western District of Virginia, in the case of Crockett v. Sorenson, 568 F.Supp. 1422, 1425-1430 (W.D. Va. 1983). Elizabeth Ridenour, Public Schools - Bible Curriculum (Greensboro, N.C.: National Council On Bible Curriculum, 1996), pp. 29-31, 42-43. Robert K. Skolrood, The National Legal Foundation, letter to National Council on the Bible Curriculum in Public

Schools, Sept. 13, 1994, pp. 3-5.

**77 The Daily Nebraskan,** April 13, 2002.

**78 Franklin, Benjamin.** William S. Pfaff, ed., Maxims and Morals of Benjamin Franklin (New Orleans: Searcy and Pfaff, Ltd., 1927).

**79 Adams, Samuel.** November 20, 1772, in his pamphlet entitled, The Rights of the Colonists, in section: "The Rights of the Colonist as Christians." The Rights of the Colonists (Boston: Old South Leaflets), Vol. VII, 1772. Adams, Writings. Selim H. Peabody, ed., American Patriotism - Speeches, Letters, and Other Papers Which Illustrate the Foundation, the Development, the Preservation of the United States of America (NY: American Book Exchange, 1880), p. 34. Charles E. Kistler, This Nation Under God (Boston: Richard T. Badger, 1924), p. 73. The Annals of America, 20 vols. (Chicago, IL: Encyclopedia Britannica, 1968), Vol. 2, pp. 218-219. Verna M. Hall, The Christian History of the Constitution of the United States of America - Christian Self-Government (San Francisco: Foundation for American Christian Education, 1976), p. xiii. Marshall Foster and Mary-Elaine Swanson, The American Covenant - The Untold Story (Roseburg, OR: Foundation for Christian Self-Government, 1981; Thousand Oaks, CA: The Mayflower Institute, 1983, 1992), p. 112. Pat Robertson, America's Dates with Destiny (Nashville: Thomas Nelson Publishers, 1986), p. 91. John Eidsmoe, Christianity and the Constitution - The Faith of Our Founding Fathers (Grand Rapids, MI: Baker Book House, A Mott Media Book, 1987; 6th printing, 1993), p. 254. "Our Christian Heritage," Letter from Plymouth Rock (Marlborough, NH: The Plymouth Rock Foundation), pp. 2, 4. Peter Marshall and David Manuel, The Glory of America (Bloomington, MN: Garborg's Heart 'N Home, 1991), 1.19. D.P. Diffine, Ph.D., One Nation Under God - How Close a Separation? (Searcy, Arkansas: Harding University, Belden Center for Private Enterprise Education, 6th edition, 1992), p. 5.

**80 Jefferson, Thomas.** 1781, in his Notes on the State of Virginia, Query XVIII, 1781, 1782, p. 237. Paul Leicester Ford, The Writings of Thomas Jefferson (New York: G.P. Putnam's Sons, the Knickerbocker Press, 1894), 3:267. A.A. Lipscomb and Albert Bergh, eds., The Writings of Thomas Jefferson 20 vols. (Washington, D.C.: The Thomas Jefferson Memorial Association, 1903-1904). Vol. IX, Vol. II, p. 227. Saul K. Padover, ed., The Complete Jefferson (New York: Tudor Publishing, 1943), p. 677. Robert Byrd, United States Senator from West Virginia, July 27, 1962, in a message delivered in Congress two days after the Supreme Court declared prayer in schools unconstitutional. Merrill D. Peterson, ed., Jefferson Writings (NY: Literary Classics of the United States, Inc., 1984) p. 289. Robert Flood, The Rebirth of America (Philadelphia: Arthur S. DeMoss Foundation, 1986), pp. 66-69. Tim LaHaye, Faith of Our Founding Fathers (Brentwood, TN: Wolgemuth & Hyatt, Publishers, Inc., 1987), pp. 192-193. George Grant, Third Time Around (Brentwood, TN: Wolgemuth & Hyatt, Inc., 1991), p. 103. D.P. Diffine, Ph.D., One Nation Under God - How Close a Separation? (Searcy, Arkansas: Harding University, Belden Center for Private Enterprise Education, 6th edition, 1992), p. 10. Gary DeMar, America's Christian History: The Untold Story (Atlanta, GA: American

Vision Publishers, Inc., 1993), p. 56. Stephen McDowell and Mark Beliles, "The Providential Perspective" (Charlottesville, VA: The Providence Foundation, P.O. Box 6759, Charlottesville, Va. 22906, January 1994), Vol. 9, No. 1, p. 5.
**81 Hamilton, Alexander.** Keith Fournier, In Defense of Liberty (Virginia Beach, VA: Law & Justice, Spring 1993), Vol. 2, No. 2, p. 7.
**82 Paine, Thomas.** December 23, 1776, in The American Crisis, No. 1. John Bartlett, Bartlett's Familiar Quotations (Boston: Little, Brown and Company, 1855, 1980), p. 384. Robert Flood, The Rebirth of America (Philadelphia: Arthur S. DeMoss Foundation, 1986), p. 16. "Common Sense" Thomas Paine - 1776 (Reston, VA: Intercessors For America, July/August 1993), Vol. 20, No. 7/8, p. 1.
**83 Truman, Harry S.** October 5, 1949, in a letter to John L. Sullivan, accepting the Honorary Chairmanship of National Brotherhood Week. T.S. Settel, and the staff of Quote, editors, The Quotable Harry Truman introduction by Merle Miller (NY: Droke House Publishers, Inc., Berkley Publishing Corporation, 1967), p. 28.
**84 United States Supreme Court. Zorach v. Clauson**, 343 US 306 307 312-314 (1952), Justice William O. Douglas. Dr. Ed Rowe, The ACLU and America's Freedom (Washington: Church League of America, 1984), pp. 20-21. Tim LaHaye, Faith of Our Founding Fathers (Brentwood, TN: Wolgemuth & Hyatt, Publishers, Inc., 1987), pp. 9-10. Martin Shapiro and Roco Tresolini, eds., American Constitutional Law (NY: Macmillan Publishing, 5th edition, 1979), p. 445. John Whitehead, The Rights of Religious Persons in Public Education (Wheaton IL: Crossway Books, Good News Publishers, 1991), p. 284. "Our Christian Heritage," Letter from Plymouth Rock (Marlborough, NH: The Plymouth Rock Foundation), p. 7. Elizabeth Ridenour, Public Schools - Bible Curriculum (Greensboro, N.C.: National Council On Bible Curriculum, 1996), p. 24.
**85 Hoover, Herbert Clark.** August 10, 1954, at a reception in honor of his eightieth birthday in West Branch, Iowa. Lillian W. Kay, ed., The Ground on Which We Stand - Basic Documents of American History (NY: Franklin Watts., Inc, 1969), p. 276-872.
**86 Eisenhower, Dwight.** February 20, 1955. Remarks broadcast from the White House as part of the American Legion "Back-To-God" Program.
**87 Reagan, Ronald Wilson.** January 13, 1993, at the Presidential Medal of Freedom Ceremony at the White House. Frederick J. Ryan, Jr., ed., Ronald Reagan - The Wisdom and Humor of The Great Communicator (San Francisco: Collins Publishers, A Division of Harper Collins Publishers, 1995), p. 19.
**88 Bush, George Walker.** January 28, 2003, State of the Union Address, Public Papers of the Presidents. www.whitehouse.gov.
**89 Rush, Benjamin.** 1798. 1786, in "Thoughts upon the Mode of Education Proper in a Republic," published in Early American Imprints. Benjamin Rush, Essays, Literary, Moral and Philosophical (Philadelphia: Thomas and Samuel F. Bradford, 1798), p. 8, "Of the Mode of Education Proper in a Republic." The Annals of America, 20 vols. (Chicago, IL: Encyclopedia Britannica, 1968), Vol. 4, pp. 28-29. Stephen McDowell and Mark Beliles, "The Providential Perspective"

(Charlottesville, VA: The Providence Foundation, P.O. Box 6759, Charlottesville, Va. 22906, January 1994), Vol. 9, No. 1, p. 3.

**90 Coolidge, (John) Calvin.** October 15, 1924, at the unveiling to the Equestrian Statue of Bishop Francis Asbury, Washington, D.C. Calvin Coolidge, Foundations of the Republic - Speeches and Addresses (New York: Charles Scribner's Sons, 1926), pp. 149-155.

**91 Henry, Patrick.** Tryon Edwards, D.D., The New Dictionary of Thoughts - A Cyclopedia of Quotations (Garden City, NY: Hanover House, 1852; revised and enlarged by C.H. Catrevas, Ralph Emerson Browns and Jonathan Edwards [descendent, along with Tryon, of Jonathan Edwards (1703-1758), president of Princeton], 1891; The Standard Book Company, 1955, 1963), p. 337.

**92 Reagan, Ronald Wilson.** August 23, 1984 at an ecumenical prayer breakfast at the Reunion Arena in Dallas, on the occasion of the enactment of the Equal Access Bill of 1984. Jeremiah O'Leary, "Reagan Declares that Faith Has Key Role in Political Life," The Washington Times (August 24, 1984). Walter Shapiro, "Politics and the Pulpit," Newsweek (September 17, 1984), p. 24. The Speech That Shook The Nation (Forerunner, December 1984), p. 12. Nadine Strossen, "A Constitutional Analysis of the Equal Access Act's Standards Governing School Student's Religious Meetings," Harvard Journal on Legislation, Winter, 1987. p. 118. David R. Shepherd, Ronald Reagan: In God We Trust (Wheaton, IL: Tyndale House Publishers, Inc., 1984), p. 146.

**93 Alabama, State of.** 1901, Constitution, Preamble. Constitutions of the United States - National and States (Dobbs Ferry, New York: Oceana Publications, Inc., published for Legislative Drafting Research Fund of Columbia University, Release 96-4, Issued November 1996), Vol. 1, Alabama, Booklet 1(March 1996), p. 1. Charles E. Rice, The Supreme Court and Public Prayer (New York: Fordham University Press, 1964), p. 167; "Hearings, Prayers in Public Schools and Other Matters," Committee on the Judiciary, U.S. Senate (87th Cong., 2nd Sess.), 1962, pp. 268 et seq. Executive Proclamations declaring "Christian Heritage Week," signed September 28, 1994, and August 13, 1993 by Governor Jim Folsom; and December 23, 1992, by Governor Guy Hunt in the city of Montgomery. Courtesy of Bruce Barilla, Christian Heritage Week Ministry (P.O. Box 58, Athens, W.V. 24712; 304-384-7707, 304-384-9044 fax).

**94 Alaska, State of.** 1956, Constitution, Preamble. Constitutions of the United States - National and State (Dobbs Ferry, New York: Oceana Publications, Inc., published for Legislative Drafting Research Fund of Columbia University, Release 95-5, Issued December 1995), Vol. 1, Alaska(June 1992), p. 1. Charles E. Rice, The Supreme Court and Public Prayer (New York: Fordham University Press, 1964), p. 167; "Hearings, Prayers in Public Schools and Other Matters," Committee on the Judiciary, U.S. Senate (87th Cong., 2nd Sess.), 1962, pp. 268 et seq.

**95 Arizona, State of.** 1912, Constitution, Preamble. Constitutions of the United States - National and State (Dobbs Ferry, New York: Oceana Publications, Inc., published for Legislative Drafting Research Fund of Columbia University, Issued

September 1993), Vol. 1, Arizona(September 1993), p. 1. Charles E. Rice, The Supreme Court and Public Prayer (New York: Fordham University Press, 1964), p. 167; "Hearings, Prayers in Public Schools and Other Matters," Committee on the Judiciary, U.S. Senate (87th Cong., 2nd Sess.), 1962, pp. 268 et seq.

**96 Arkansas, State of.** 1874, Constitution, Preamble. Frances Newton Thorpe, ed., Federal and State Constitutions, Colonial Charters, and Other Organic Laws of the States, Territories, and Colonies now or heretofore forming the United States, 7 vols. (Washington: Government Printing Office, 1905; 1909; St. Clair Shores, MI: Scholarly Press, 1968). Constitutions of the United States - National and State (Dobbs Ferry, New York: Oceana Publications, Inc., published for Legislative Drafting Research Fund of Columbia University, Release 94-4, Issued October 1994), Vol. 1, Arkansas(October 1994), p. 1. Charles E. Rice, The Supreme Court and Public Prayer (New York: Fordham University Press, 1964), p. 167; "Hearings, Prayers in Public Schools and Other Matters," Committee on the Judiciary, U.S. Senate (87th Cong., 2nd Sess.), 1962, pp. 268 et seq. Miller, The First Liberty - Religion and the American Republic, p. 109. Gary DeMar, "God and the Constitution" (Atlanta, GA: Biblical Worldview, An American Vision Publication - American Vision, Inc., December 1993), p. 11. Cited August 21, 1996, in an Executive Proclamation declaring November 24 - November 30, 1994, as "Christian Heritage Week," signed by Governor Mike Huckabee and Secretary of State Sharon Priest. Courtesy of Bruce Barilla, Christian Heritage Week Ministry (P.O. Box 58, Athens, W.V. 24712; 304-384-7707, 304-384-9044 fax).

**97 California, State of.** 1849, Constitution, Preamble. Constitutions of the United States - National and State (Dobbs Ferry, New York: Oceana Publications, Inc., published for Legislative Drafting Research Fund of Columbia University, Release 96-4, Issued November 1996), Vol. 1, California(November 1996), p. 1. Charles E. Rice, The Supreme Court and Public Prayer (New York: Fordham University Press, 1964), p. 168; "Hearings, Prayers in Public Schools and Other Matters," Committee on the Judiciary, U.S. Senate (87th Cong., 2nd Sess.), 1962, pp. 268 et seq.

**98 Colorado, State of.** 1876, Constitution, Preamble. Constitutions of the United States - National and State (Dobbs Ferry, New York: Oceana Publications, Inc., published for Legislative Drafting Research Fund of Columbia University, Issued October 1992), Vol. 1, Colorado(October 1992), p. 1. Charles E. Rice, The Supreme Court and Public Prayer (New York: Fordham University Press, 1964), p. 168; "Hearings, Prayers in Public Schools and Other Matters," Committee on the Judiciary, U.S. Senate (87th Cong., 2nd Sess.), 1962, pp. 268 et seq.

**99 Connecticut, State of.** 1818, Constitution, Preamble. Frances Newton Thorpe, ed., Federal and State Constitutions, Colonial Charters, and Other Organic Laws of the States, Territories, and Colonies now or heretofore forming the United States, 7 vols. (Washington: Government Printing Office, 1905; 1909; St. Clair Shores, MI: Scholarly Press, 1968). Charles E. Rice, The Supreme Court and

Public Prayer (New York: Fordham University Press, 1964), p. 168; "Hearings, Prayers in Public Schools and Other Matters," Committee on the Judiciary, U.S. Senate (87th Cong., 2nd Sess.), 1962, pp. 268 et seq. Gary DeMar, "God and the Constitution," (Atlanta, GA: The Biblical Worldview, An American Vision Publication, American Vision, Inc., December 1993). William Miller, The First Liberty - Religion and the American Republic (NY: 1986), p. 109.

**100 Delaware, State of.** 1897, Constitution, Preamble. Frances Newton Thorpe, ed., Federal and State Constitutions, Colonial Charters, and Other Organic Laws of the States, Territories, and Colonies now or heretofore forming the United States, 7 vols. (Washington: Government Printing Office, 1905; 1909; St. Clair Shores, MI: Scholarly Press, 1968). Charles E. Rice, The Supreme Court and Public Prayer (New York: Fordham University Press, 1964), p. 168; "Hearings, Prayers in Public Schools and Other Matters," Committee on the Judiciary, U.S. Senate (87th Cong., 2nd Sess.), 1962, pp. 268 et seq. Edwin S. Gaustad, Neither King nor Prelate - Religion and the New Nation, 1776-1826 (Grand Rapids, MI: William B. Eerdmans Publishing Company, 1993), pp. 161-162. Gary DeMar, God and Government, A Biblical and Historical Study (Atlanta, Georgia: American Vision Press), Vol. 1, pp. 164-165. Church of the Holy Trinity v. U.S., 143 U.S. 457, 469-470. Recorded in The State of Delaware Executive Proclamation of November 14 - 20, 1993, as "Christian Heritage Week," signed by Governor Thomas R. Caper, and Lieutenant Governor Ruth Ann Minner. Courtesy of Bruce Barilla, Christian Heritage Week Ministry (P.O. Box 58, Athens, W.V. 24712; 304-384-7707, 304-384-9044 fax).

**101 Florida, State of.** 1885, Constitution, Preamble. Frances Newton Thorpe, ed., Federal and State Constitutions, Colonial Charters, and Other Organic Laws of the States, Territories, and Colonies now or heretofore forming the United States, 7 vols. (Washington: Government Printing Office, 1905; 1909; St. Clair Shores, MI: Scholarly Press, 1968), Vol. II, p. 733. Charles E. Rice, The Supreme Court and Public Prayer (New York: Fordham University Press, 1964), p. 168; "Hearings, Prayers in Public Schools and Other Matters," Committee on the Judiciary, U.S. Senate (87th Cong., 2nd Sess.), 1962, pp. 268 et seq. Anson Phelps Stokes and Leo Pfeffer, Church and State in the United States (NY: Harper and Row, Publishers, 1950, revised one-volume edition, 1964), p. 156.

**102 Georgia, State of.** 1777, Constitution, Preamble. Charles E. Rice, The Supreme Court and Public Prayer (New York: Fordham University Press, 1964), p. 169; "Hearings, Prayers in Public Schools and Other Matters," Committee on the Judiciary, U.S. Senate (87th Cong., 2nd Sess.), 1962, pp. 268 et seq. Benjamin Weiss, God in American History: A Documentation of America's Religious Heritage (Grand Rapids, MI: Zondervan, 1966), p. 155. Gary DeMar, America's Christian History: The Untold Story (Atlanta, GA: American Vision Publishers, Inc., 1993), p. 65.

**103 Hawaii, State of.** 1959, Constitution, Preamble. Charles E. Rice, The Supreme Court and Public Prayer (New York: Fordham University Press, 1964),

p. 169; "Hearings, Prayers in Public Schools and Other Matters," Committee on the Judiciary, U.S. Senate (87th Cong., 2nd Sess.), 1962, pp. 268 et seq. Recorded in an Executive Proclamation declaring February 12 - 22, 1994, as "Christian Heritage Week," signed by Governor John Waihee, in the Capitol City of Honolulu, December 30, 1993. Courtesy of Bruce Barilla, Christian Heritage Week Ministry (P.O. Box 58, Athens, W.V. 24712; 304-384-7707, 304-384-9044 fax).

**104 Idaho, State of.** 1889, Constitution, Preamble. Charles E. Rice, The Supreme Court and Public Prayer (New York: Fordham University Press, 1964), p. 169; "Hearings, Prayers in Public Schools and Other Matters," Committee on the Judiciary, U.S. Senate (87th Cong., 2nd Sess.), 1962, pp. 268 et seq. Recorded in the Executive Proclamation declaring October 16 - 22, 1994, as "Christian Heritage Week," signed in the Capitol City of Boise by Governor Cecil D. Andrus and Secretary of State Pete T. Cenarrusa. Courtesy of Bruce Barilla, Christian Heritage Week Ministry (P.O. Box 58, Athens, W.V. 24712; 304-384-7707, 304-384-9044 fax).

**105 Illinois, State of.** 1870, Constitution, Preamble. Charles E. Rice, The Supreme Court and Public Prayer (New York: Fordham University Press, 1964), p. 169; "Hearings, Prayers in Public Schools and Other Matters," Committee on the Judiciary, U.S. Senate (87th Cong., 2nd Sess.), 1962, pp. 268 et seq. Church of the Holy Trinity v. United States 143 U.S. 457, (1892). Gary DeMar, God and Government-A Biblical and Historical Study (Atlanta: GA: American Vision Press, 1984), p. 143.

**106 Indiana, State of.** 1851, Constitution, Preamble. Charles E. Rice, The Supreme Court and Public Prayer (New York: Fordham University Press, 1964), p. 169; "Hearings, Prayers in Public Schools and Other Matters," Committee on the Judiciary, U.S. Senate (87th Cong., 2nd Sess.), 1962, pp. 268 et seq.

**107 Iowa, State of.** 1857, Constitution, Preamble. Charles E. Rice, The Supreme Court and Public Prayer (New York: Fordham University Press, 1964), p. 169; "Hearings, Prayers in Public Schools and Other Matters," Committee on the Judiciary, U.S. Senate (87th Cong., 2nd Sess.), 1962, pp. 268 et seq.

**108 Kansas, State of.** 1859, Constitution, Preamble. Charles E. Rice, The Supreme Court and Public Prayer (New York: Fordham University Press, 1964), pp. 169-170; "Hearings, Prayers in Public Schools and Other Matters," Committee on the Judiciary, U.S. Senate (87th Cong., 2nd Sess.), 1962, pp. 268 et seq.

**109 Kentucky, State of.** 1891, Constitution, Preamble. Charles E. Rice, The Supreme Court and Public Prayer (New York: Fordham University Press, 1964), p. 170; "Hearings, Prayers in Public Schools and Other Matters," Committee on the Judiciary, U.S. Senate (87th Cong., 2nd Sess.), 1962, pp. 268 et seq. Executive Proclamation by Governor Brereton C. Jones and Secretary of State Robert Babbage, declaring November 21 - November 27, 1993, as "Christian Heritage Week," signed November 1, 1993, in the Capitol City of Frankfort.

Courtesy of Bruce Barilla, Christian Heritage Week Ministry (P.O. Box 58, Athens, W.V. 24712; 304-384-7707, 304-384-9044 fax).

**110 Louisiana, State of.** 1921, Constitution, Preamble. Charles E. Rice, The Supreme Court and Public Prayer (New York: Fordham University Press, 1964), p. 170; "Hearings, Prayers in Public Schools and Other Matters," Committee on the Judiciary, U.S. Senate (87th Cong., 2nd Sess.), 1962, pp. 268 et seq.

**111 Maine, State of.** 1819, Constitution, Preamble. Charles E. Rice, The Supreme Court and Public Prayer (New York: Fordham University Press, 1964), p. 170; "Hearings, Prayers in Public Schools and Other Matters," Committee on the Judiciary, U.S. Senate (87th Cong., 2nd Sess.), 1962, pp. 268 et seq.

**112 Maryland, State of.** 1776, Constitution, Preamble. Benjamin Weiss, God in American History: A Documentation of America's Religious Heritage (Grand Rapids, MI: Zondervan, 1966), p. 155. Gary DeMar, America's Christian History: The Untold Story (Atlanta, GA: American Vision Publishers, Inc., 1993), p. 65.

**113 Massachusetts, State of.** 1780, Constitution, Preamble. Henry Steele Commager, ed., Documents of American History, 2 vols. (NY: F.S. Crofts and Company, 1934; Appleton-Century-Crofts, Inc., 1948, 6th edition, 1958; Englewood Cliffs, NJ: Prentice Hall, Inc., 9th edition, 1973), Vol. I, pp. 107-108. The Annals of America, 20 vols. (Chicago, IL: Encyclopedia Britannica, 1968), Vol. I, pp. 322-333. Jacob C. Meyer, Church and State in Massachusetts from 1740-1833 (Cleveland: Western Reserve Press, 1930) pp. 234-235. Anson Phelps Stokes and Leo Pfeffer, Church and State in the United States (NY: Harper and Row, Publishers, 1950, revised one-volume edition, 1964), p. 77. The Constitutions of All the United States According to the Latest Amendments (Lexington, KY: Thomas T. Skillman, 1817), p. 89. The Constitutions of the Several Independent States of America (Philadelphia: Bailey, published by order of the U.S. Continental Congress, 1781, in the Evans Collection, #17390), p. 138. Gary DeMar, "Censoring America's Christian History" (Atlanta, GA: The Biblical Worldview, An American Vision Publication - American Vision, Inc., July 1990), p. 7. Benjamin Weiss, God in American History: A Documentation of America's Religious Heritage (Grand Rapids, MI: Zondervan, 1966), p. 155. Gary DeMar, America's Christian History: The Untold Story (Atlanta, GA: American Vision Publishers, Inc., 1993), p. 65. Frances Newton Thorpe, ed., Federal and State Constitutions, Colonial Charters, and Other Organic Laws of the States, Territories, and Colonies now or heretofore forming the United States, 7 vols. (Washington: Government Printing Office, 1905; 1909; St. Clair Shores, MI. Scholarly Press, 1968), Vol. V, p. 38.

**114 Michigan, State of.** 1908, Constitution, Preamble. Charles E. Rice, The Supreme Court and Public Prayer (New York: Fordham University Press, 1964), p. 171; "Hearings, Prayers in Public Schools and Other Matters," Committee on the Judiciary, U.S. Senate (87th Cong., 2nd Sess.), 1962, pp. 268 et seq.

**115** **Minnesota, State of.** 1857, Constitution, Preamble. Charles E. Rice, The Supreme Court and Public Prayer (New York: Fordham University Press, 1964), p. 171; "Hearings, Prayers in Public Schools and Other Matters," Committee on the Judiciary, U.S. Senate (87th Cong., 2nd Sess.), 1962, pp. 268 et seq.

**116** **Mississippi, State of.** 1890, Constitution, Preamble. Charles E. Rice, The Supreme Court and Public Prayer (New York: Fordham University Press, 1964), pp. 171-172; "Hearings, Prayers in Public Schools and Other Matters," Committee on the Judiciary, U.S. Senate (87th Cong., 2nd Sess.), 1962, pp. 268 et seq.

**117** **Missouri, Constitution of the State of.** 1945, Preamble. Charles E. Rice, The Supreme Court and Public Prayer (New York: Fordham University Press, 1964), p. 172; "Hearings, Prayers in Public Schools and Other Matters," Committee on the Judiciary, U.S. Senate (87th Cong., 2nd Sess.), 1962, pp. 268 et seq.

**118** **Montana, State of.** 1889, Constitution, Preamble. Charles E. Rice, The Supreme Court and Public Prayer (New York: Fordham University Press, 1964), p. 172; "Hearings, Prayers in Public Schools and Other Matters," Committee on the Judiciary, U.S. Senate (87th Cong., 2nd Sess.), 1962, pp. 268 et seq.

**119** **Nebraska, State of.** June 12, 1875, Constitution, Preamble. Charles E. Rice, The Supreme Court and Public Prayer (New York: Fordham University Press, 1964), p. 172; "Hearings, Prayers in Public Schools and Other Matters," Committee on the Judiciary, U.S. Senate (87th Cong., 2nd Sess.), 1962, pp. 268 et seq.

**120** **Nevada, State of.** 1864, Constitution, Preamble. Charles E. Rice, The Supreme Court and Public Prayer (New York: Fordham University Press, 1964), p. 172; "Hearings, Prayers in Public Schools and Other Matters," Committee on the Judiciary, U.S. Senate (87th Cong., 2nd Sess.), 1962, pp. 268 et seq.

**121** **New Hampshire, State of.** 1784, 1792, Part One, Article I, Section V. The Constitutions of All the United States According to the Latest Amendments (Lexington, KY: Thomas T. Skillman, 1817), pp. 27, 29. The Constitutions of the Several Independent States of America, Published by Order of Congress (Boston: Norman & Bowen, 1785) p. 3-4. Frances Newton Thorpe, ed., Federal and State Constitutions, Colonial Charters, and Other Organic Laws of the States, Territories, and Colonies now or heretofore forming the United States, 7 vols. (Washington: Government Printing Office, 1905; 1909; St. Clair Shores, MI: Scholarly Press, 1968). Charles E. Rice, The Supreme Court and Public Prayer (New York: Fordham University Press, 1964), p. 172; "Hearings, Prayers in Public Schools and Other Matters," Committee on the Judiciary, U.S. Senate (87th Cong., 2nd Sess.), 1962, pp. 268 et seq. New Hampshire Manuel (1937), pp. 9-10.5. Edwin S. Gaustad, Neither King nor Prelate - Religion and the New Nation, 1776-1826 (Grand Rapids, MI: William B. Eerdmans Publishing Company, 1993), p. 166.

**122** **New Jersey, State of.** 1844, 1947, Constitution, Preamble. Charles E. Rice, The Supreme Court and Public Prayer (New York: Fordham University Press, 1964), pp. 172-173; "Hearings, Prayers in Public Schools and Other Matters," Committee on the Judiciary, U.S. Senate (87th Cong., 2nd Sess.), 1962, pp. 268

et seq. Tim LaHaye, Faith of Our Founding Fathers (Brentwood, TN: Wolgemuth & Hyatt, Publishers, Inc., 1987), p. 92.

**123** **New Mexico, State of.** 1911, Constitution, Preamble. Charles E. Rice, The Supreme Court and Public Prayer (New York: Fordham University Press, 1964), p. 173; "Hearings, Prayers in Public Schools and Other Matters," Committee on the Judiciary, U.S. Senate (87th Cong., 2nd Sess.), 1962, pp. 268 et seq.

**124** **New York, State of.** 1846, Constitution, Preamble. Frances Newton Thorpe, ed., Federal and State Constitutions, Colonial Charters, and Other Organic Laws of the States, Territories, and Colonies now or heretofore forming the United States, 7 vols. (Washington: Government Printing Office, 1905; 1909; St. Clair Shores, MI: Scholarly Press, 1968). Charles E. Rice, The Supreme Court and Public Prayer (New York: Fordham University Press, 1964), p. 173; "Hearings, Prayers in Public Schools and Other Matters," Committee on the Judiciary, U.S. Senate (87th Cong., 2nd Sess.), 1962, pp. 268 et seq. Benjamin Weiss, God in American History: A Documentation of America's Religious Heritage (Grand Rapids, MI: Zondervan, 1966), p. 155. Tim LaHaye, Faith of Our Founding Fathers (Brentwood, TN: Wolgemuth & Hyatt, Publishers, Inc., 1987), p. 93. Gary DeMar, America's Christian History: The Untold Story (Atlanta, GA: American Vision Publishers, Inc., 1993), p. 66. Gary DeMar, "Censoring America's Christian History" (Atlanta, GA: The Biblical Worldview, An American Vision Publication - American Vision, Inc., July 1990).

**125** **North Carolina, State of.** 1868, Constitution, Preamble. Charles E. Rice, The Supreme Court and Public Prayer (New York: Fordham University Press, 1964), p. 173; "Hearings, Prayers in Public Schools and Other Matters," Committee on the Judiciary, U.S. Senate (87th Cong., 2nd Sess.), 1962, pp. 268 et seq.Tim LaHaye, Faith of Our Founding Fathers (Brentwood, TN: Wolgemuth & Hyatt, Publishers, Inc., 1987), p. 92.

**126** **North Dakota, State of.** 1889, Constitution, Preamble. Charles E. Rice, The Supreme Court and Public Prayer (New York: Fordham University Press, 1964), p. 173; "Hearings, Prayers in Public Schools and Other Matters," Committee on the Judiciary, U.S. Senate (87th Cong., 2nd Sess.), 1962, pp. 268 et seq.

**127** **Ohio, State of.** 1852, Constitution, Preamble. The Constitutions of the United States of America with the Latest Amendments (Trenton: Moore & Lake, 1813), p. 334. Frances Newton Thorpe, ed., Federal and State Constitutions, Colonial Charters, and Other Organic Laws of the States, Territories, and Colonies now or heretofore forming the United States, 7 vols. (Washington: Government Printing Office, 1905; 1909; St. Clair Shores, MI: Scholarly Press, 1968). Charles E. Rice, The Supreme Court and Public Prayer (New York: Fordham University Press, 1964), pp. 173-174; "Hearings, Prayers in Public Schools and Other Matters," Committee on the Judiciary, U.S. Senate (87th Cong., 2nd Sess.), 1962, pp. 268 et seq.

**128** **Oklahoma, State of.** 1907, Constitution, Preamble. Charles E. Rice, The Supreme Court and Public Prayer (New York: Fordham University Press, 1964),

p. 174; "Hearings, Prayers in Public Schools and Other Matters," Committee on the Judiciary, U.S. Senate (87th Cong., 2nd Sess.), 1962, pp. 268 et seq.

**129 Oregon, State of.** 1857, Constitution, Bill of Rights, Article I, Section 2. Charles E. Rice, The Supreme Court and Public Prayer (New York: Fordham University Press, 1964), p. 174; "Hearings, Prayers in Public Schools and Other Matters," Committee on the Judiciary, U.S. Senate (87th Cong., 2nd Sess.), 1962, pp. 268 et seq.

**130 Pennsylvania, State of.** 1776, Constitution, Preamble. Charles E. Rice, The Supreme Court and Public Prayer (New York: Fordham University Press, 1964), p. 174; "Hearings, Prayers in Public Schools and Other Matters," Committee on the Judiciary, U.S. Senate (87th Cong., 2nd Sess.), 1962, pp. 268 et seq. Benjamin Weiss, God in American History: A Documentation of America's Religious Heritage (Grand Rapids, MI: Zondervan, 1966), p. 155. Gary DeMar, America's Christian History: The Untold Story (Atlanta, GA: American Vision Publishers, Inc., 1993), p. 65.

**131 Rhode Island and Providence Plantations, State of.** 1842, Constitution, Preamble. Charles E. Rice, The Supreme Court and Public Prayer (New York: Fordham University Press, 1964), p. 174; "Hearings, Prayers in Public Schools and Other Matters," Committee on the Judiciary, U.S. Senate (87th Cong., 2nd Sess.), 1962, pp. 268 et seq. Benjamin Weiss, God in American History: A Documentation of America's Religious Heritage (Grand Rapids, MI: Zondervan, 1966), p. 155. Tim LaHaye, Faith of Our Founding Fathers (Brentwood, TN: Wolgemuth & Hyatt, Publishers, Inc., 1987), p. 92. Gary DeMar, America's Christian History: The Untold Story (Atlanta, GA: American Vision Publishers, Inc., 1993), pp. 64-64.

**132 South Carolina, State of.** 1778, Constitution, Preamble. Frances Newton Thorpe, ed., Federal and State Constitutions, Colonial Charters, and Other Organic Laws of the States, Territories, and Colonies now or heretofore forming the United States, 7 vols. (Washington: Government Printing Office, 1905; 1909; St. Clair Shores, MI: Scholarly Press, 1968). Charles E. Rice, The Supreme Court and Public Prayer (New York: Fordham University Press, 1964), pp. 174-175; "Hearings, Prayers in Public Schools and Other Matters," Committee on the Judiciary, U.S. Senate (87th Cong., 2nd Sess.), 1962, pp. 268 et seq. Benjamin Weiss, God in American History: A Documentation of America's Religious Heritage (Grand Rapids, MI: Zondervan, 1966), p. 155. Gary DeMar, "Censoring America's Christian History" (Atlanta, GA: The Biblical Worldview, An American Vision Publication - American Vision, Inc., July 1990), p. 7. Gary DeMar, America's Christian History: The Untold Story (Atlanta, GA: American Vision Publishers, Inc., 1993), p. 66.

**133 South Dakota, State of.** 1889, Constitution, Preamble. Charles E. Rice, The Supreme Court and Public Prayer (New York: Fordham University Press, 1964), p. 175; "Hearings, Prayers in Public Schools and Other Matters," Committee on the Judiciary, U.S. Senate (87th Cong., 2nd Sess.), 1962, pp. 268 et seq.

**134 Tennessee, State of.** 1796, Constitution, Article XI, Section 3. Frances Newton Thorpe, ed., Federal and State Constitutions, Colonial Charters, and Other Organic Laws of the States, Territories, and Colonies now or heretofore forming the United States, 7 vols. (Washington: Government Printing Office, 1905; 1909; St. Clair Shores, MI: Scholarly Press, 1968). Edwin S. Gaustad, Neither King nor Prelate - Religion and the New Nation, 1776-1826 (Grand Rapids, MI: William B. Eerdmans Publishing Company, 1993), pp. 172-73. Governor Ned McWherter and Secretary of State Riley C. Darnell, Proclamation declaring Christian Heritage Week, August 29 - September 4, 1993, signed June 21, 1993, in the Capitol City of Nashville. Courtesy of Bruce Barilla, Christian Heritage Week Ministry (P.O. Box 58, Athens, W.V. 24712; 304-384-7707, 304-384-9044 fax).

**135** **Texas, State of.** August 27, 1845, Constitution, Preamble. Journals of the Convention, Assembled at the City of Austin on the Fourth of July, 1845, for the purpose of framing a Constitution for the State of Texas (Austin, TX: Miner & Cruger, Printers to the Convention, 1845; A Facsimile Reproduction of the 1845 Edition with a Preface by Mary Bell Hart, Shoal Creek Publishers, 1974), p. 338.

**136** **Utah, State of.** 1896, Constitution, Preamble. Charles E. Rice, The Supreme Court and Public Prayer (New York: Fordham University Press, 1964), p. 175; "Hearings, Prayers in Public Schools and Other Matters," Committee on the Judiciary, U.S. Senate (87th Cong., 2nd Sess.), 1962, pp. 268 et seq.

**137** **Vermont, State of.** July 8, 1777, Constitution. Perley Poore, ed., The Federal and State Constitutions, Colonial Charters, and Other Organic Laws of the United States (Washington, 1877), Vol. II, p. 1857. Frances Newton Thorpe, ed., Federal and State Constitutions, Colonial Charters, and Other Organic Laws of the States, Territories, and Colonies now or heretofore forming the United States, 7 vols. (Washington: Government Printing Office, 1905; 1909; St. Clair Shores, MI: Scholarly Press, 1968). The Annals of America, 20 vols. (Chicago, IL: Encyclopedia Britannica, 1968), Vol. 2, p. 483.

**138** **Virginia, State of.** July 12, 1776; 1830; 1851; 1868; 1902; 1928, Constitution, Bill of Rights, Article I, Section 16. Frances Newton Thorpe, ed., Federal and State Constitutions, Colonial Charters, and Other Organic Laws of the States, Territories, and Colonies now or heretofore forming the United States, 7 vols. (Washington: Government Printing Office, 1905; 1909; St. Clair Shores, MI: Scholarly Press, 1968), Vol. VII, p. 3814. Benjamin Franklin Morris, The Christian Life and Character of the Civil Institutions of the United States (Philadelphia, PA: L. Johnson & Co., 1863; George W. Childs, 1864), p. 232. Henry Steele Commager, ed., Documents of American History, 2 vols. (NY: F.S. Crofts and Company, 1934; Appleton-Century-Crofts, Inc., 1948, 6th edition, 1958; Englewood Cliffs, NJ: Prentice Hall, Inc., 9th edition, 1973), pp. 103-104. Charles Fadiman, ed., The American Treasury (NY: Harper & Brothers, Publishers, 1955), p. 121. Charles E. Rice, The Supreme Court and Public Prayer (New York: Fordham University Press, 1964), pp. 175-176; "Hearings, Prayers in Public Schools and Other Matters," Committee on the Judiciary, U.S. Senate (87th Cong., 2nd Sess.), 1962, pp. 268 et seq. The Annals of America, 20 vols.

(Chicago, IL: Encyclopedia Britannica, 1968), Vol. 2, p. 433. Pat Robertson, America's Dates with Destiny (Nashville: Thomas Nelson Publishers, 1986), pp. 80-81. "Our Christian Heritage," Letter form Plymouth Rock (Marlborough, NH: The Plymouth Rock Foundation), p. 3. Stephen McDowell and Mark Beliles, "The Providential Perspective" (Charlottesville, VA: The Providence Foundation, P.O. Box 6759, Charlottesville, Va. 22906, January 1994), Vol. 9, No. 1, p. 2. Edwin S. Gaustad, Neither King nor Prelate - Religion and the New Nation, 1776-1826 (Grand Rapids, MI: William B. Eerdmans Publishing Company, 1993), p. 174.

**139 Washington, State of.** 1889, Constitution, Preamble. Charles E. Rice, The Supreme Court and Public Prayer (New York: Fordham University Press, 1964), p. 176; "Hearings, Prayers in Public Schools and Other Matters," Committee on the Judiciary, U.S. Senate (87th Cong., 2nd Sess.), 1962, pp. 268 et seq.

**140 West Virginia, State of.** 1872, Constitution, Preamble. Charles E. Rice, The Supreme Court and Public Prayer (New York: Fordham University Press, 1964), p. 176; "Hearings, Prayers in Public Schools and Other Matters," Committee on the Judiciary, U.S. Senate (87th Cong., 2nd Sess.), 1962, pp. 268 et seq.

**141 Wisconsin, State of.** 1848, Constitution, Preamble. Charles E. Rice, The Supreme Court and Public Prayer (New York: Fordham University Press, 1964), p. 176; "Hearings, Prayers in Public Schools and Other Matters," Committee on the Judiciary, U.S. Senate (87th Cong., 2nd Sess.), 1962, pp. 268 et seq. Governor Tommy G. Thompson and Secretary of State Douglas La Follet, Proclamation of Christian Heritage Week October 3 - October 9, 1993, in the Capitol City of Madison. A similar Proclamation was also signed November 1, 1994. Courtesy of Bruce Barilla, Christian Heritage Week Ministry (P.O. Box 58, Athens, W.V. 24712; 304-384-7707, 304-384-9044 fax).

**142 Wyoming, State of. 1890,** Constitution, Preamble. Charles E. Rice, The Supreme Court and Public Prayer (New York: Fordham University Press, 1964), p. 176; "Hearings, Prayers in Public Schools and Other Matters," Committee on the Judiciary, U.S. Senate (87th Cong., 2nd Sess.), 1962, pp. 268 et seq.

**143 United States Presidential Addresses upon assuming office.** Public Papers of the Presidents (Washington, D.C.: United States Government Printing Office.)

CPSIA information can be obtained
at www.ICGtesting.com
Printed in the USA
JSHW012132130720
6672JS00001B/31

9 780975 345511